# *Contents*

So aftir thes questis of Syr Gawayne Syr
Tor and kynge Pellynore than hit befelle that Merlyon felle in dotage on the damesell that kynge Pellynore
brought to courte and she was one of the damesels of the lady of the
laake that hyght Nenyve But Merlion wolde nat lette her have
no reste but all wayes he wolde be wyth her And ever she made
Merlion good chere tylle she had lerned of hym all maner of thyng
that she desyred and he was assoted uppon hir that he
myght nat be from hir So on a tyme he tolde to kynge
Arthure that he scholde nat endure longe but for all
his craft he scholde be putte in to the erthe quyk and so
he tolde the kyng many thyngis that scholde be falle
but all wayes he warned the kyng to kepe well his swer-
de and the scawberde scholde be stolyn by a woman frome
hym that he moste trusted Also he tolde kyng Arthure
that he scholde mysse hym And yett had ye levir than all
youre londis have me agayne I sayde the kyng syn ye
knowe of youre evil adventure purvey for hit and putt
hit a way by youre craufft that mysse adventure Nay seyde
he hit wolt not be he departed frome the kyng And within
a whyle the damesell of the lake departed and Merlyon
went with her evirmore where som evir she yeode and oftyn ty-
mes he wolde have had hir prevayly away by his subtyle
craufft Than she made hym to swere that he scholde neu do
none inchauntemente uppon hir if he wolde have his will
And so he swore Than she and Merlyon wente ou the see un
to the londe of Benwyke there as kyng Ban was kyng
that had grete warre ayenste kyng Claudas And there
Merlyon spake wt kyng Bans wyff a fayre lady and a good hir
name was Elayne And there he sawe younge Launcelot
And there the queene made grete sorowe for the mortal
werre that kyng Claudas made on hir londis Take

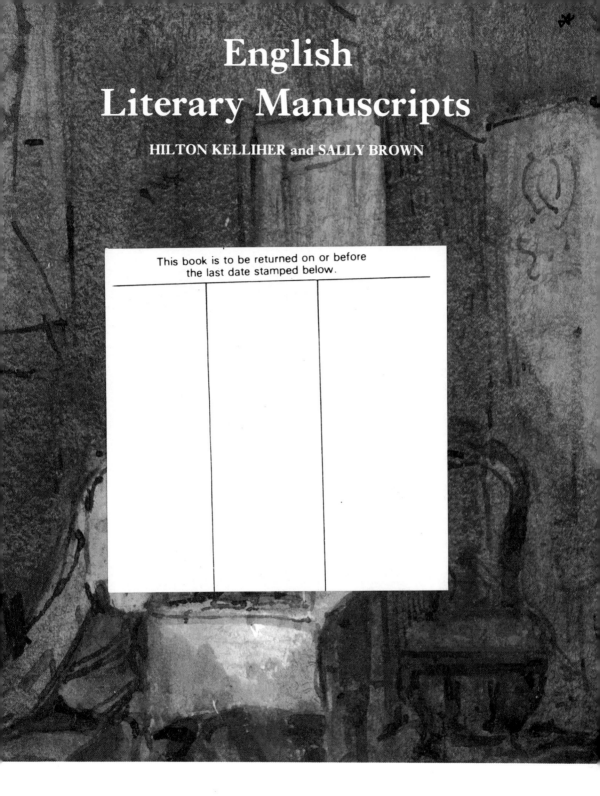

# English
# Literary Manuscripts

### HILTON KELLIHER and SALLY BROWN

This book is to be returned on or before
the last date stamped below.

## The British Library

© 1986 The British Library Board
Reprinted 1995

Published by
The British Library
Great Russell Street
London WC1B 3DG

BL British Library Cataloguing
in Publication Data

Kelliher, Hilton
  English literary manuscripts.
  1. English literature—
  Manuscripts—Catalogs
  I. Title   II. Brown, Sally   III.
  British Library
  016.8208      Z6611.L7
  ISBN 0-7123-0117-8

Designed by Roger Davies
Typeset in Monophoto Ehrhardt
by August Filmsetting, Haydock,
St Helens
Origination by York House
Graphics, Hanwell
Printed in England by
Clifford Press Ltd, Coventry

relevant point in Hoccleve's poem,
shows him in later life, a rather portly
fair-haired man with a ruddy
complexion and a forked beard.
[Harley MS 4866, f.88]

*Back Cover*: James Joyce (1882–1941)
*Finnegans Wake*.
This is a draft, from a notebook
written in 1823–24, of part of Joyce's
second great work, which was first
published as a whole in 1939. With its
predecessor, *Ulysses*, it revolutionised
the form and structure of the novel.
[Add. MS 47471 B, f.70]

*Title page*: William Makepeace
Thackeray (1811–1863): watercolour
sketch of a tavern scene.
[Add. MS 46908, f.5]

*This page*: Dora Carrington
(1893–1932): Letter to Lytton
Strachey.
'Carrington', as she was always
known, first met Strachey in 1915 and
remained devoted to him until his
death in 1932, soon after which she
took her own life. Many of her letters
to him are illustrated with impromptu
sketches, like this one, dated 1916.
[Add. MS 62888, ff.72v–73]

*This page*: Thomas Babington
Macaulay (1800–1859).
Watercolour sketch, by an unknown
artist, of Macaulay in the Manuscripts
Room of the British Museum.
[Egerton MS 3803]

# Introduction

The purpose of this book is to give some idea of the richness and variety of the national collection of English literary manuscripts. As a representative body of material drawn from the whole course of imaginative literature written in English in Britain the holdings of the British Library cannot be matched elsewhere. They range in date from the earliest specimens of Anglo-Saxon to drafts of work by living authors. They include manuscripts by Scottish, Irish and Welsh writers, such as Robert Burns, James Joyce and Dylan Thomas. They cover every variety of prose, verse and drama. And they embrace every possible type of literary document, from medieval illuminated texts and autograph fair copies to annotated typescripts and corrected proofs. As a result, they are of interest equally as much to the editor and textual critic as to the literary historian, the biographer and the student of handwriting.

That this collection of English literary manuscripts should have such a range is hardly surprising, for it is founded on a series of private libraries each of which is rich in some particular period or field. This is not the place to attempt a summary of the contents of the four great collections that were combined in the British Museum Library in 1759 – those, that is, of Sir Robert Cotton, Sir Hans Sloane, Robert and Edward Harley, 1st and 2nd Earls of Oxford, and the Old Royal Library formed by successive monarchs from Edward VI to George II. They were supplemented, during the first thirty years of the 19th century, by a further half-dozen collections of distinction. In our own century the George Murray Smith Bequest and the purchase of the Ashley Library of the bibliographer T. J. Wise have added enormously to our holdings of manuscripts of writers from the Romantics to Conrad. Many modern literary autographs were acquired through a scheme set up jointly with the Arts Council of Great Britain in 1964 (since discontinued); while, following the Theatres Act of 1968, the British Library now has responsibility for copies of all English plays performed in the United Kingdom since 1824, and formerly lodged with the Lord Chamberlain.

In view of Britain's historical connections with India, it is not surprising that correspondence of literary men is also to be found in the India Office Library and Records, which became part of the British Library in 1982. Naturally, the main collection, which is preserved in the Department of Manuscripts, is being increased all the while by purchase and gift.

Some of the manuscripts illustrated in the following pages have interesting, even extraordinary, histories. Two of the very finest, both belonging to the later 15th century, were discovered quite independently in 1934. The autobiography of Margery Kempe turned up in a cupboard of household oddments, while the owner was searching for ping-pong balls; and the unique manuscript of Malory's *Morte d'Arthur* was discovered in the Fellows' Library at Winchester College where it may have lain unrecognised since the early 17th century. The famous 'Percy Folio' of English ballads was found in about 1750 by Thomas Percy during a visit to a friend's house where the maid was using it to light the fire – hence the missing or mutilated leaves at its beginning.

1 Sir Thomas Malory (died 1471): *Le Morte d'Arthur*. The sole-surviving manuscript of Malory's vast compilation of Arthurian legends was copied at some time during the 1470s or early 1480s. It is the work of two scribes, the hand of the principal or supervising scribe being seen in the first six lines of this page.
[Add. MS 59678, f.45]

The charred covers of Traherne's *Commentaries of Heaven* tell a similar story. This was rescued from a burning rubbish-tip in south Lancashire around 1967. The finder subsequently emigrated to Canada, where the manuscript was identified in 1980, the latest in a series of discoveries of unsuspected manuscripts of Traherne. A trunk of papers uncovered in a London bank-vault in 1976 turned out to have belonged to Lord Byron's friend, Scrope Davies. When the contents were examined they were found to include – amongst the bills, betting-slips and other memorabilia – poems by both Byron and Shelley that Davies had undertaken to carry from Italy to England. They had been abandoned when his mounting debts forced him to flee the country early in 1820. The number and frequency of such discoveries over the past half-century offers a very strong likelihood of more to come.

It might be as well at this stage to consider what is meant by literary manuscripts. In the strictest sense, of course, they are handwritten texts of works of creative literature, such as *Beowulf* or *Le Morte d'Arthur*; the revised fair copy of the play of *Sir Thomas More*; Browne's drafts for *Urne-buriall* and Pope's for his translation of the *Iliad*; or Dickens's *Nicholas Nickleby* and the note-books of W. H. Auden. Many pieces of imaginative writing never intended for publication, like Pepys's Diary, Coleridge's notebooks and marginalia, or the letters of Edward Lear, undoubtedly also deserve to be included. By the same token one may admit non-fictional or philosophical masterpieces such as Hobbes's *Leviathan*, Gibbon's *Autobiography* or Sassoon's *Memoirs of a Fox-Hunting Man*, for these have become part of the English literary heritage. But there are other types of document that may be considered as literary manuscripts – namely, almost any handwritten item deriving from or relating to a writer and his work, or to the production and publication of that work. This brings in, besides modern typewritten drafts and revised proofs, the records of the 16th- and 17th-century Masters of the Revels, business letters of certain Victorian publishers, and even the drawings with which Keith Douglas proposed to illustrate his *Alamein to Zem Zem*.

Something should also be said of the terms used in describing literary manuscripts. First, the word 'autograph' means quite simply 'written in the hand of the author of the work'; the autograph fair copy of Gray's *Elegy* is therefore that which was copied by himself. Clearly, a man's own signature must be autograph; but to speak of 'an autograph' as if it denotes a signature is a misuse of the term, perpetuated in works like *The Guinness Book of Autographs*, which is exclusively a collection of signatures of famous people in facsimile. Perhaps this growing misconception is attributable to the popularity of 'autograph-albums'. Another term that is sometimes rather loosely used as a synonym for 'autograph' is 'holograph', which actually means 'written wholly in the hand of one man' and should not be taken to imply that the hand is that of the author. In the progress of a work from script to print, an autograph draft usually belongs to an earlier stage of composition than an autograph fair copy. Later still comes the typewritten copy of modern times – though some writers have been known to move from manuscript to typescript and back to manuscript – and finally the printed proof with autograph corrections or revisions. The distinction to be drawn between these two last terms is also an important one.

The aspect of manuscripts that probably intrigues people most is their handwriting, the historical study of which is called palaeography. The history of handwriting shows a definite line of development, discernible in the illustrations in this book. Simply stated, the various styles of hand – the common abbreviation for handwriting – developed partly as a result of outside influences, such as imitation of foreign models, and partly in response to the practical necessities of copying. The formal book-hands, as they are called, that are found in manuscripts of Chaucer's age, developed for ease and speed of copying in a growing commercial market into the cursive styles practised during the 15th-century. From the hands of the two Malory scribes of the 1470s to that of Sir Thomas Wyatt in the 1530s is only a short step; and this Tudor cursive gave rise to the Secretary hand that reached its peak during the reigns of Elizabeth I and James I.

At the same time there appeared the Roman or Italic style, originating from Italian humanist hands and very widely taught by writing-masters. Examples may be found in the handwriting of Donne and Milton. This Italic, simpler in form and therefore quicker to learn and write than its rival, offers few difficulties to the modern reader, while the Secretary abounds in unfamiliar letter-forms. Among these may be mentioned the reversed 'e', the 'h' looped beneath the line, and the long 's' resembling an 'f' that are seen in the hand of *Sir Thomas More* and, later, in that of Sir Thomas Browne. Other notable features include abbreviations like 'ye' for 'the', in which the initial 'th' has been replaced by the similarly-sounded Old English runic letter called 'thorn' ( þ ). From this comes our entirely spurious expression 'ye olde. . .'. It was not unusual, however, for scribes or authors to practise both of these hands, sometimes in the same document. Many others wrote what is basically one of these styles, though with features borrowed from the other: this resulted in a 'mixed' hand, such as those of Ralegh or Jonson.

During the 18th century, writing-masters began to teach a new round hand that is sometimes called 'copperplate'. In due course this became universally accepted as the 'English hand'; its influence may be traced in Jane Austen and Charles Lamb. In the 19th century, aided somewhat by the invention of the steel-nibbed pen in the 1820s, handwriting began to develop along more individualistic lines that tend to defy categorisation. Once again speed, at this time of widespread literacy, was the catalyst; and the pace of politics, business and journalism had the direst consequences for legibility. It was this general decline in standards that led, in the early years of the 20th century, to a movement for better handwriting, and in particular for the revival of the Italic hand. The result can be seen in the clear and careful hands practised by Sassoon and Douglas.

Apart from their interesting hands, or their value as literary relics, what kinds of information can be gathered from manuscripts? For the period before the invention of printing they are, of course, supremely important as witnesses to the text, and indeed the very existence, of the works that they preserve. Even after Caxton they retain their textual value whenever the work concerned did not get into print, or when it was printed after the author's death, or merely without his active supervision. The importance of the many verse-commonplace books surviving from the 16th and 17th centuries lies in the means that they provide of checking the accuracy, and identifying the authorship, of poems that were never seen through the press, or in constructing a pedigree – known as a 'stemma' – for assessing the relative value of the surviving texts of a poet's work. With autograph or similar material, early drafts have been found to shed valuable light on the processes of composition, and even to supply clues to the author's meaning in obscure passages.

Sometimes a considerable amount of useful information may be derived from studying the make-up of a manuscript that comprises several different physical 'layers'. The printer's manuscript of Wordsworth's *Poems, in Two Volumes* (1807), which was copied out by members of his household and sent to the publisher in packets through the post over a period of some six months, is a case in point. From the various papers and hands that compose it we can infer the existence, and even the contents, of an earlier manuscript of poems that had been dismembered for partial re-use here and that supplies a missing link in the development of Wordsworth's shorter poems. We can recover the exact shape and extent of the single volume that was initially agreed with the publisher in the autumn of 1806. And we can trace every step of the printing, piecemeal as it was, noting Wordsworth's changes in proof and seeing how the final product in some ways failed to match up to his intentions. Furthermore, it enables us to learn something about the composition-dates of several of the poems that were included.

Finally, it must be emphasised that the information to be derived from a manuscript is seldom exhausted. The most meticulous edition or photographic-facsimile cannot reproduce all the details of the original. As our knowledge grows about an author and his methods, and as new techniques of scientific examination are developed, so fresh questions suggest themselves and new avenues of approach open up. We cannot, however, anticipate what these may be, and it is therefore essential that we spare no effort in preserving and recording our manuscripts, since any aspect of their physical make-up, however trivial it may seem to us, may be the subject of fruitful research and literary discoveries in the future.

# From the beginnings to 1500

The written records of Old English, as the language of the Anglo-Saxons is nowadays called, include the largest quantity of creative literature to have come down to us from the early Middle Ages in any language except Latin. As with all older literatures, its most significant and highly-developed aspect is its poetry. While native Anglo-Saxon prose begins only with the revival of learning fostered by King Alfred of Wessex (848–899), the earliest oral poetry is sometimes considerably older. The anonymous epic of *Beowulf*, which celebrates the exploits of a 6th-century Scandinavian hero, probably belongs to the following century. Its unique manuscript (2), which dates from roughly 1000 AD, seems to owe its existence to a general impulse towards the systematic preservation of specimens of Old English poetry. The Cotton Library fire of 1731 that charred its margins and damaged or destroyed other contemporary works reminds us that Anglo-Saxon literature must have sustained many similar losses throughout the ages.

*Beowulf* was composed in the Germanic measure known as alliterative verse, which depends on stress and the internal rhyming of initial sounds, rather than on the syllable-counting and end-rhymes familiar to us since the time of Chaucer.

Hwaet we Gardena ingear-dagum ...     [*Beowulf*, line 1]

or later:

In a somere seyson · whan softe was the sonne ... [*Piers Plowman*, line 1]

When English, in its newly-modified form, finally reasserted itself over the Latin and Norman-French of the post-Conquest period, this native tradition of verse-writing was revived. From the second half of the 14th century two alliterative masterpieces survive. The romance of *Sir Gawain and the Green Knight* (4) appears to derive from Cheshire or south Lancashire, and the manuscript in which it is preserved is remarkable as the earliest surviving attempt to illustrate any mediaeval English poem. Very different in character is the social and religious allegory of Langland's *Piers Plowman* (3), the three successive versions of which are represented by no fewer than seventy contemporary manuscripts.

Literary works copied in the hands of their authors are rarely met with before the 16th century. The enormous success of Langland's topical poem marks the virtual beginning of professional copying of English literary works on a large scale; by the end of the century the growing demand for copies was being satisfied by an increasing number of full-time scribes. These craftsmen carried out commissions for wealthy patrons or for the stationers who acted both as publishers and booksellers. As occasion demanded they could turn out relatively plain texts on high-quality papers that had recently begun to be imported from the Continent, or sumptuous manuscripts on vellum.

Alliterative verse soon gave way to the rhymed syllabic variety that was naturalised from French and Italian models by Chaucer and his friend John Gower, a London lawyer whose poems still survive in upwards of seventy manuscripts, including some fine presentation-copies. The scribe of the *Confessio* (6) was a professional copyist whose large and well-spaced hand is closely matched by that found in one (5) of the five complete manuscripts of Geoffrey Chaucer's *Canterbury Tales* surviving in the Harley collection. Chaucer's great poem, which has come down to us in over eighty contemporary copies, remained uncompleted at his death; and in the absence of an autograph or other clearly authorial versions Chaucer's intentions have to be inferred from comparison of all the different texts. This manuscript presents a unique ordering of the tales, with some evidence of intelligent editing by an unknown hand.

The copyist of the *Tales* was a prolific craftsman who around the turn of the 15th century produced handsome collections of poetry by Langland, Chaucer and Gower; the decoration was left, as was customary, to skilled painters. The portrait of Chaucer found in the Harley manuscript of Thomas Hoccleve's *Regimen of Princes* (**front cover**) was certainly the work of such an independent artist, though as a likeness it was presumably approved by Hoccleve, who had been a friend of Chaucer. Interestingly enough, the scribe of the Chaucer manuscript is known to have collaborated at some time with Hoccleve and others in copying a manuscript of Gower's *Confessio* that is now in Cambridge. As a Clerk of the Privy Seal Hoccleve was an expert penman who was evidently happy to supplement his income by occasional work of this kind.

From the 13th century, cycles of short 'Mystery Plays' on biblical subjects had been performed in towns and cities by guilds of tradesmen on religious feast-days. Most of the surviving manuscripts belong to the latter part of the 15th century. The dialect of the so-called 'N-Town Plays' (8), which were at one time thought to originate from Coventry, points rather to the East Midlands. This paper manuscript, smaller in format than the other surviving cycles and carefully corrected in various hands, may have been the property of a travelling company of players.

Two English prose-works of the 15th century stand out from the rest. Margery Kempe of King's Lynn, whose autobiography (7) is only the second known book by an Englishwoman, was (like most people at this time) illiterate. She dictated the first version of her memoirs to a friend who could write. The present manuscript, which belongs to the decade or so following her death in about 1439, stands at two removes from the earliest one.

But the greatest literary achievement of the age is undoubtedly the vast compilation of Arthurian romances adapted largely from French by Sir Thomas Malory of Newbold Revel, much of whose adult life was passed in prison, as punishment for various unchivalric misdemeanours. The unique manuscript (1) has in the course of its history lost the first and last quires of its original 1,000 pages of text.

The presence of faint offset type-letters on some pages of the Malory manuscript suggests that it had been in Caxton's office at Westminster while he was printing *Le Morte d'Arthur* (1485). And so, ironically enough, it seems to have been used by the very man who brought into England the craft by which the professional copying of finely-written and illuminated literary texts was soon to be superseded.

**2** *Beowulf*: about 1000 AD This anonymous 7th-century epic is the earliest surviving poem in a major European language and one of the few specimens of Germanic heroic poetry known to us. The unique manuscript was copied on vellum several centuries later than the composition and was damaged by fire in 1731.
[Cotton MS Vitellius A XV, f.133]

...ende þagyt hie him asetton segen...

denne heah ofer heafod leton holm ber

gearfon ongaf seg him þæt geomor sef

murnende mod men ne cunnon secgan

sode sele rædenne hæleð under heofen

hwa þæm hlæste onfeng.

Ða wæs on burgum beowulf scyldinga leo
leod cyning longe þrage folcum gefræ
ge ræder ellor hwearf aldor of earde
oð þ him eft onwoc heah healf dene heold
þenden lifde gamol ⁊ guð reouw glæde scyl
dingas ðæm feower bearn forð gerimed in
worold wocun weoroda ræswa heoro gar ⁊
hroð gar ⁊ halga til hyrde ic þelan cwen
heaðo scilfingas heals gebedda þa wæs hroð
gare here sped gyfen wiges weorð myrð þ
him his wine magas georne hyrdon oð þ
seo geo god geweox mago driht micel h
on mod bearn þ hal reced hatan wolde

11

Among crystene creatures · þif crystes wordþ be tȝelþe·······
Dabo tibi seđm peticionem tuam·
¶What is pfit pacience·qnos Actiua uita·
Mekenesse anð mylde speche· anð men of on wil
þe whiche wile loue leðe·to oure lorðes place
anð þat is charite chaumpion·chef of alle veytues·······
¶Anð þat is pore pacience·alle pereles to suffre
wheþer pouerte anð pacience·plece more god al myȝti
þan so rithful richesse·anð resonableli to speuðe·······
¶Je quis est·ille qnos concience·qub lauðabimus ev
þalþ men reðen of richesse· rith to þe worlðes enðe
anð whan he ðron hun to þe ðey·þat he ne ðrat hun saye
þan eny pore pacient· anð þat i preue bi resoun·······
¶Þit ayn but felþe folt of þe riche·þat ne falleþ in a ȝelage
þer þe pore say pleðe· anð preue be pyne reson
To haue a lonaunce of his lorð· bi lawþe he clayme þ iore
þat neueȝe iore he haðde·of rithful inȝe he askeþ
anð sey lo haðdes anð bestes·þat no iore knowþen
anð wilde wermes in wodes· in wyntez þolþ hem greueth
anð makest hem wel meke· anð mylðe for ðefaute
After þolþ senðest hem somer· þat is heore souereȝin iore
anð blisse to alle þat ben· boþe wilðe anð tame·······
¶þanne man beggeþ as bestes· after blisse aþþe
þat al heore lyf han i lyues· in languoz anð ðefaute
But goð senðe hem tine· of sum maney iore
Oþer here oz elles wheze· elles weȝe hit uyþe
ffoz to woreþhele was he wrouþt·þat neueȝe was iore shapen·······
¶Angeles þat noþ in helle ben·haðden sum tune iore
anð ðiues in ðentþuous lyuyng· anð in ðouce nie
anð noþ he bnyþey hit ful bittere·he is a beggeþ in helle·······
¶Many men han heore iore here·for al heore welðeðes
anð lorðes anð laðies ben calð·for leðes þat þei hauen
anð flexey as hit semey·anð somey eneȝe hem folewþeþ·······
¶Whan ðey awakey hem of heore wele·þat weȝen here so riche
þanne ayn þei pine pore þynges·in purgatorue oz in helle
þauiþ in þe sautter· of swiche makey mynðe····-·····
anð sey ðormieȝint ꝉ michil ineneȝint ꝉ iciu velus soþnu siiȝ·
    Hic incipit passus septimus de ðolwel·········
        Las þat richesse schal reue· oz robbe manes soule
        ffoz þe loue of oure lorð· at his laste enðe
        þei þat nouþ han bi foren·anð ayn eneȝe moze pore

**3** William Langland (about 1332–about 1400): *The Vision of Piers Plowman*.
Three separate versions of Langland's allegorical poem were composed between about 1362 and 1390. This is a copy of the final or 'C'-Text, and was transcribed about 1390–1400. Each of the alliterative verses is marked by a red point at the break of the line.
[Cotton MS Vespasian B XVI, f.64v]

**4** *Sir Gawain and the Green Knight*: about 1400 AD
The manuscript of this aliterative romance on an Arthurian theme is almost the earliest illustrated work of literature in English. This rather crudely-drawn sketch represents the temptation of Gawain by the wife of his opponent.
[Cotton MS Nero A X, f.129]

**5** (Overleaf) Geoffrey Chaucer (about 1340–1400): 'The Friar's Tale' from *The Canterbury Tales*.
The scribe of this handsome vellum manuscript of about 1410 was one of the most prolific copyists of vernacular texts in this period. The decorative initial with elaborate three-quarter border that is seen on the right-hand page was added by another artist.
[Harley MS 7334, ff. 102v, 103]

4

Sith I may gouern and chese as me list
Ye certis Wyf quod he I hold it best
Kys me quod sche we ben no lenger Wrope
ffor by my trouthe I Wol be to yow bope
This is to say ye bope fair and good
I pray to god pat I mot sterue Wood
But I be to yow also good and treWe
As euer Was Wyf sippen pe World Was neWe
And but I be to moroW as fair to seen
As eny lady empesse or queen
That is bitWixe thest and eek pe West
Doth by my lyf right euen as yoW lest
Cast op pe cortyns and look What pis is
And Whan pe knyght saugh verraply al pis
That sche so fair Was and so yong perto
ffor ioye he hent hir in hir armes tuo
his herte bathid in a bath of blisse
A thousand tyme on roWe he gan hir kisse
And sche obeyed him in euery ping
That mighte doon him pleisauns or likyng
And pus pay lyue vnto her lyues ende
In parfit ioye and ihū crist vs sende
housbondes meke yonge and freissche on bedde
And grace to ouerbyye hem pat We Wedd
And eek I pray to ihū sthort her lyues
That Wil nought be gouerned after her Wyues
And old and angry nygardes of despense
God send hem sone verray pestilence

Here endith pe Wif of Bathe hire tale .
There bygyneth pe plog of pe ffreres tale .
This Worthy lymytour pie noble ffreir
He made alWay a lourynge cheere
Vpon the sompnо̄ but for honeste
No vileyns Worde yit to him spak he
But atte last he sayd vnto pe Wyf
Dame quod he god yiue yoW good lyf
ye han her touchid also mot I the
In scole mater grett difficulte

14

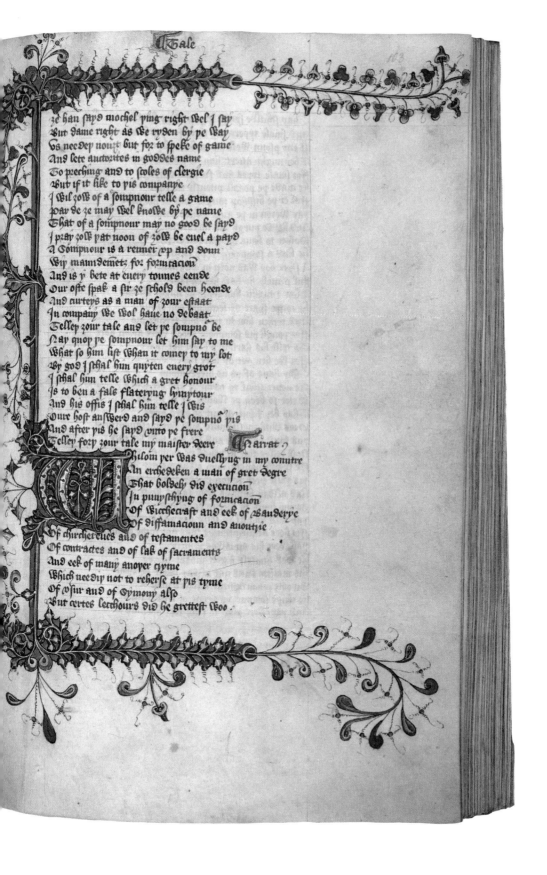

ze han sayd mochel ping right wel I say
But dame right as we ryden by pe way
vs needep nouzt but for to speke of game
And lete auctorites in goddes name
To preching and to scoles of clergie
But if it like to pis companye
I wil zow of a sompnour telle a game
Par de ze may wel knowe by pe name
That of a sompnour may no good be sayd
I pray zow pat noon of zow be euel a payd
A Sompnour is a renner vp and doun
Wip maundementz for fornicacioun
And is y bete at euery tounes eende
Our ofte spak a sir ze schold been heende
And curteys as a man of zour estaat
In company we wol haue no debaat
Tellep zour tale and let pe sompno̅ be
Nay quop pe sompnour let him say to me
What so him list whan it comep to my lot
By god I schal him quyten euery grot
I schal him telle which a gret honour
Is to ben a fals flateryng lymytour
And his offis I schal him telle I wis
Oure host answerd and sayd pe sompno̅ pis
And after pis he sayd vnto pe frere
Tellep forp zour tale my maister deere

¶ Narrat

Hilom per was duellyng in my countre
An erchedeken a man of gret degre
That boldely did execucion
In punysshyng of fornicacion
Of wicchecraft and eek of baudeye
Of diffamacioun and auoutrie
Of chircherittes and of testamentes
Of contractes and of lak of sacramentes
And eek of many anoper cryme
Which needip not to reherse at pis tyme
Of vsur and of Symony also
But certes lecchours did he grettest wo

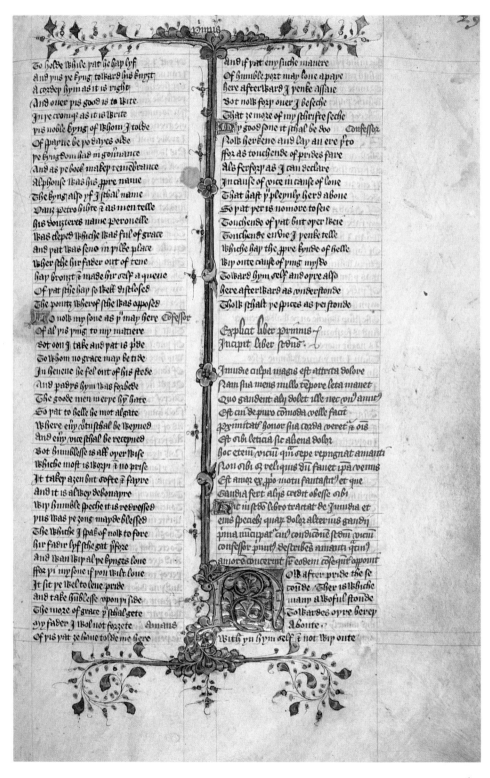

To holde while þat he hap lyf
And þus þe kyng tolward his knyzt
A corded hym as it is right
And ouer þis good is to write
In þe cronic as it is write
þis noble kyng of whom I tolde
Of sparne be þe dayes olde
þe kyngdom had in gouernance
And as þe book makeþ remembrance
Alphonse was his apre name
The kyng also yf I schal name
Daun Petro sibire & as men telle
his douzteres name Peronelle
was clepes whiche was ful of grace
And þat was seno in pilke place
Wher sche hir fader out of tene
hay brozt & made hir self a queene
Of þat sche hap so wel enclosed
The pointz wherof sche was oposed

Lo now my sone as þ may here    Confessor
Of al þis þing to my matiere
Bot oon I take and þat is pride
To whom no grace may be tide
In heuene he fel out of his stede
And þadis hym was forbede
The goode men merye hy hate
So þat to helle he mot algate
Where euy contr schal be weyned
And euy vice schal be receyned
Bot humblesse is aff oþer wise
whiche most is worþ & no prise
It takeþ azen but softe & fayre
And it is alwey debonayre
Wiþ humble speche it is redressed
þus was þe zong mayde blessed
The whiche I spak of now to fore
hir fadir lyf sche gat þforse
And þan Wiþ al þe kynges loue
ffor þi my sone if þou wilt loue
It sit þe wel to leue pride
And take humblesse vpon þi side
The more of grace þ schalt gete
My fader I wol not forzete    Amans
Of þis þat ze haue tolde me here

And if þat eny suche manere
Of humble port may loue apaye
here afterward I þenke assaie
Bot now forþ ouer I beseche
That ze more of my schrifte seche

My good sone it schal be doo    Confessor
Now herkene and lay an ere þto
ffor as touchende of prides fare
Als ferforþ as I can declare
In cause of vice in cause of loue
That hast þ pleynly herd aboue
So þat þer is nomore to seie
Touchende of þat but oþer weie
Touchende enuie I þenke telle
whiche hap the apre kynde of helle
Wiþoute cause of ryng myzdo
Toward hym self and oþre also
here afterward as vnderstonde
Now schalt þe spices as þei stonde

Explicit liber primus
Incipit liber secundus

Inuidia culpa magis est attrita dolore
Nam sua mens nullo tempore leta manet
Quo gaudent alij dolet ille nec cõuidunt amici
Est an de puro cõmoda velle fiat
Proximitas honor sua corda veret & ois
Est sibi letiaú sic aliena dolor
Hoc etem viciú qm sepe repugnat amanti
Non sibi qz reliquis dum fauet ipa venus
Est amor ex ppo motu fantasiú et que
Gaudia fert alijs credit obesse sibi

Hic in isto libro tractat de Inuidia et
eius speciebz quaz dolor alterius gaudij
pma nuncupat cui conditione scdm ouem[?]
confessor puurj[?] describes amantis gquo[?]
amore concernut se eodem cõsequi apponit

Now after pride the se
toude  Ther is whiche
many a woful stonde
Towardes oþre berey
Aboute
Wiþ yn hym self & not wiþ oute

Here begynnyth a schort tretys and a comfortabyl for synful wrecchys, wher in þei may haue gret solas and comfort to hem, and vndyrstondyn þe hy & vnspecabyl mercy of ower souereyn Sauyowr cryst Ihesu, whos name be worschepd and magnyfyed wythowtyn ende, þat now in ower days to vs vnworthy deyneth to exercysen hys nobeley & hys goodnesse. Alle þe werkys of ower Sauyowr ben for ower exampyl & instruccyon, and what grace þat he werkyth in any creatur is ower profyth yf lak of charyte be not ower hynderawnce. And þerfor, be þe leue of ower mercyful Lord Cryst Ihesu, to þe magnyfying of hys holy name Ihesu, þis lytyl tretys schal tretyn sumdeel in parcel of hys wonderful werkys, how mercyfully, how benyngly, & how charytefully he meued & stered a synful caytyf vn to hys loue. Whech synful caytyf many zerys was in wyl and in purpose thorw steryng of þe holy gost to folwyn sauyowr, makyng gret behestys of fastyngys wyth many oþer dedys of penawnce. And euyr sche was turned a zen a bak in tym of temptacyon, leech vn to þe reed spyr, whech bowyth wyth euery wynd & neuyr is stable. Les þan no wynd blowyth. On to þe tyme þat ower mercyfulle Lord cryst Ihesu hauyng pety & compassyon of hys hand werke & hys creatur turnyd helth in to sekenesse, prosperyte in to aduersyte, worschep in to repref & loue in to hatered. Thus alle þys thyngys turnyng vp so down, þys creatur whych many zerys had gon wyl & euyr ben vnstable, was parfythly drawen & steryd to entren þe wey of hy perfeccyon. Whech parfyth wey cryst ower sauyowr in hys propyr persoone examplyd. Sadly he trad it & dewly he went it be forn. Than þus creatur of whom þys tretys thorw þe mercy of Ihesu schal schewen in party þe leuyng, whech be ye hand of ower

Angelus ad pastores ait. Glia in excelsis deo.

Pax to god þ syt in heuyn
And pees to man on erþe grolynde
A chylde is born to vothe þ kynn
thynke hym many folke yul be vn bonnde
Sacramentys þ yul be vij.

Commyn <del> þ</del> childyr bounde
Therfor I synge a joyful stevene
þ flonys of frencheþ nolt is fennde
God þ bronght an hyze

he is glonyed mannys gost to kynne
he hath sent salue to mannys synne
pees is conne to mannys kynne
thynke goddys _____ _____

Mannyas mannyas ffolalte myrne
I balt a gynt lyght ww þyne
Zit salt mobyr so vell þyne
Chappyn vpon þ skyes

It is bynghtor yan þ sunne bem
It comyth pyght ow all yor yorn
Glynn aboue bedleem
I salt it byorne thynee

Zen art my brothor boskes
I haue be holdyn þ same pas
I thynke it is þ tokonynge of gyas

9

8 The 'N-Town Cycle' of Mediaeval Mystery Plays: late 15th century.
Though formerly identified with Coventry, this cycle is nowadays thought to
have originated in the East Midlands. The large Arabic '16' in the right-hand
margin indicates the position of this play in the sequence, while the square
brackets mark out the rhyme-scheme.
[Cotton MS Vespasian D VIII, f.88v]

9 'Westron wynde when wyll thou blowe': early 16th century.
This brief love-lyric, surviving in a musical setting that may date from shortly
after 1503, supplies a link between the 15th and 16th centuries; it belongs to the
former, in spirit if not in date of composition.
[Royal MS Appendix 58, f.5]

# The 16th and 17th Centuries

William Shakespeare
(1564–1616): Signature from
the Blackfriars mortgage-
deed, 11 March 1613.
[Egerton MS 1787 (detail)]

Throughout the greater part of these two glorious centuries, although printing continued to flourish, manuscripts remained the principal means for introducing literary works to a wide public. Poets like Sidney, Ralegh, Donne and Herrick acquired considerable reputations during their own lifetimes almost entirely through circulation of their poetry in this way. At a time, therefore, when 'publication' was still not synonymous with distribution in printed form, and when it was considered gentlemanly to show indifference to seeing one's work in print, private anthologies in manuscript are often the best witnesses to what an author actually wrote. The Elizabethan and Stuart periods are the great age of the 'commonplace book', that catch-all in which students, courtiers and members of the literate middle class jotted down poems, prose extracts, proverbs, jests and whatever else came their way. Much of the prose of these centuries survives also in numerous copies turned out by professional scribes; while drama, too, is well represented in manuscript, though few of the most famous playwrights are nowadays known by autograph examples of their craft.

Occasionally we are fortunate enough to possess authorial drafts or fair copies from this period. Sir Thomas Wyatt kept a notebook (10) in which fair copies of poems entered by an amanuensis are supplemented by a few autograph drafts. This, the primary source for his poetry, is also the earliest such notebook of any major poet that has survived, and was in use from some time before 1537 until his death in 1542. No such document is known to have come down from the next generation of poets, such as Sidney and Spenser, though Sir Walter Ralegh has left scattered autograph versions of his poems. One of these (12) was jotted down on the last leaf of a notebook that he kept, while a prisoner in the Tower, for his *History of the World* (1614). Though copied after the death of Elizabeth I, this poem belongs to a sequence that he addressed to her during her lifetime.

Without any doubt, the most desirable of all literary autographs must be a specimen of Shakespeare's dramatic work. A strong case has been made for his having revised an older play of *Sir Thomas More*, in collaboration with Munday, Chettle, Heywood and Dekker, between about 1593 and 1601, and having – like them – written out his own contribution (11). Nevertheless this case rests as much, if not more, on literary resemblances to his known work as on palaeographical considerations. For of the six surviving 'signatures' it is not known for sure which are genuine and which merely scribal proxies; nor is there any certainty that Shakespeare was even in London when the Blackfriars mortgage (see the illustration above) was drawn up.

The collections of the British Library include a large proportion of the surviving thirty-six or so contemporary manuscript anthologies devoted largely to the poems of John Donne. These are vitally important to the study of texts and attributions, since the collected edition of *Poems* (1633) was printed only after his death, by his son. A distinction should be made here between a commonplace collection, which includes examples of work by many writers, and a miscellany, which concentrates largely on a single author. The Stowe manuscript (14), incorporating copies of 102 poems by Donne, belongs to the latter class. A specimen of Donne's own hand is seen in the letter (13) in which, seeking to use his confinement to its best advantage, he asks Sir Robert Cotton for the loan of papers relating to the 'french negotia[t]ions'. This may refer to documents abstracted by Cotton from state archives, which caused his library to be confiscated by Charles I in 1629.

Donne and Jonson were the founders of two different schools of poetry, though Jonson is better known as a dramatist. His presentation-copy to Prince Henry, who died prematurely in 1612, of one of his many Court masques (15) has survived in the Old Royal Library, and for a literary man it is an unusually fine specimen of penmanship. A prominent figure among the poets who looked to Jonson as their 'father' was Robert Herrick, many of whose lyrics, though not printed until 1648, are found in commonplace books. The formal elegy (16) that he wrote as a Cambridge undergraduate on the death of a law-don from a neighbouring college came to light only recently.

John Milton's commonplace book (17) preserves, under alphabetical headings, some fruits of his reading between his leaving Cambridge in 1632 and printing *Paradise Lost* in 1667. The final entry on the page shown here was added by an amanuensis, probably after Milton became totally blind in 1652. Shortly before this calamity occurred he wrote his name in the album (18) of Christopher Arnold, Professor of History at Nuremburg, who was visiting London. The idea of an *album amicorum* ('album of friends') originated in Germany during the previous century and was widely used for collecting mementos of academic and other distinguished contacts made while abroad.

A great many of the anonymous ballads of these centuries have been preserved for us in the large collection (20) discovered by Bishop Percy (1729–1811). The 'Percy Folio' supplied a quarter of the texts in his pioneering *Reliques of Ancient English Poetry* (1765), though he took considerable liberties with his originals.

The notebooks (19) of Sir Thomas Browne, the greatest prose-stylist of the 17th century, survive among the collections assembled by another physician, Sir Hans Sloane. Browne's spiky hand frequently presents problems to editors. Thomas Traherne, who was not recognised for the superlative prose-writer and poet that he is until the early years of this century, attempted a vast encyclopaedia of moral and religious topics. The completed portion of these *Commentaries of Heaven* (21) extends, however, only as far as the beginning of the letter B. This period is brought to a close by John Dryden, the greatest dramatist, poet and critic of his age. The interesting letter (22) in which he demands his arrears of salary as Poet Laureate to Charles II is one of some eighty of his letters that have come down to us.

10

10 Sir Thomas Wyatt (about 1503–1542): Autograph verses to the river Tagus. In the summer of 1539, when recalled by Henry VIII as Ambassador to Spain, Wyatt entered this poem in his notebook. It begins 'Tagus fare well th*at* westward w*ith* thy strems ...'
[Egerton MS 2711, f.69]

11 William Shakespeare (1564–1616): Assumed autograph contribution to the play of *Sir Thomas More*.
Comparison of Shakespeare's surviving signatures with the regular Secretary hand of this passage, and the style of the dramàtic writing, has led to the supposition that it is an autograph and dates from between 1593 and 1601.
[Harley MS 7368, f.9]

oth

why eaten are you what
for to the king god eat is so god
oth dread oft Justyce powre and
they bid this while stand with of no shape
and to add magesty whilst to this
p and thus not the only lose that but the king
this the which the lord, but the fie fie and and while
shall this be god or earth, was the king
whose name the which would the earth infinity
but wish this god, which do we to the nobles
in done this o desperate and as you and
was your shold my hand and the fine fine
the the which would the which the proud
lift up for peace, and your consciences the
they made you your let to knele to be forgiven

~~[struck through lines]~~

not the which be which the which could rebell
as much which are proud, by the name
you still the not not pride though the traytor
or the not voice and parliament stand
whose is in advice let the noble
to quietness to noble, which the down the trangers
let them not begin their with the which the kings
and take the which oft laws in them
to the god her in God, find the king
as he is clemence, this this proud moved

~~[struck]~~ so much sorrow of your great trespass
can the to being which whether would the noise
which down by the altitude of the owner
shold gyve you father go which the strangers or handes
to any forreine come to france or portugale
any man which they not theres to england
which the which needs be strangers, which they graspe
to find a nation oft such, barbarous furyon
this inhumanity out in hideous violance
would not afford you, in shape on earth
which their detested charge against the which
should the which her doors, and like as the which god
owed not our world not which, nor the the should the
nor not all appropriate to god the property
but the which unto them, which would the which
to be the which, this is the strangers case
and this your mountainish inhumanity

faith he said who lett and as we were be do on this
would be will by the mayster moore of yeild stand and
should depend our selfe

submit which to these noble gentlemen
entreat their mediation to the king
gyve up the self to forme obay the magistrat
and there no doubt but mercy may be find

9

23

Now we have present made
To Cynthia, Phæbe, Flora
Diana, and Aurora.
Bewty that cannot vade.

A flower of loves owne plantinge
A patern kept, by nature
for bewty, forme, & stature
when shee would frame a darlinge

Shee is the valley of porue
whose somer ever lastethe
tyme conqueringe all thee madnes
by beinge allwayes new.

As elementall fier  //
whose food & flame consumes not
or as thee passion ends not
of vertues new desire.

So her celestiall frame
and quintessentiall minde
...  heavens togethor bynde
shall ever be the same;

Then to her servaunts leve her
love, nature & affection
printes of worldes affection
or prayses butt derebe her.

If love could finde a quill
drawen from an angells winge
or did the muses singe
yat prety wantons will.

If beautye her could indyte
to please all other sens
butt loves & woes experi
Sorroe tam only write

13

12 Sir Walter Ralegh (about 1552–1618): Autograph verses to Elizabeth I.
Ralegh's verses to 'Cynthia' – his courtly name for the Queen – are preserved at
the end of a notebook that he kept between 1603 and 1614, while a prisoner in
the Tower.
[Add. 57555, f.172v]

13 John Donne (1572–1631): Letter to Sir Robert Cotton.
On 20 February 1602, while in confinement following his secret marriage with
Anne More, Donne asks Cotton for the loan of some papers for private study.
[Cotton MS Julius C III, f.153]

# Dreame:

Deare Loue, for nothinge lesse then thee
would I haue broke this happie dreame.
It was a theame
For reason, much too stronge for fantasie,
Therefore thou wakedst me wisely, yet.
My dreame thou brok'st not, but continuedst it.
Thou art soe true, that thoughts of thee suffice
To make dreames truth and fable histories;
Enter these armes. for since thou thoughtst it best
Not to dreame all my dreame, lets doe the rest.

As lightninge, or a papers light
Thine eyes, and not thy noise awaked me.
yet I thought thee
For thou louest truth) an Angell at first sight
But when I saw thou saw'st my hart
And knewst my thoughts beyond an Angells art
When thou knewst what I dreamt, when thou knewst, when
Excesse of ioye would wake me and camest then
I doe confesse, it could not chuse but bee
Profanenes to thinke thee any thinge but thee.

Comminge and stayinge shewd thee, thee.
But risinge makes me doubt it now
Thou art not thou.
That Loue is weake where feares are stronge as hee,
Tis not all spirit pure and braue
If mixture it of feare, shame, honour haue.
Perchance as torches which must ready bee
Men light, and put out, so thou dost with mee.
thou cam'st to kindle, goest to come then I
Will dreame that hope againe, but ell would dye.

**14** Manuscript miscellany of poems by Donne: about 1623–about 1633.

Donne's poem 'The Dreame' comes from a contemporary miscellany of his verse that was copied in a fine Italic hand in the decade before the posthumous edition of his *Poems* appeared.

[Stowe MS 961, f.63]

**15** Ben Jonson (about 1572–1637): Dedication of his *Masque of Queens*.

Jonson himself wrote this presentation-copy of the masque that he had composed for the New Year festivities at Whitehall Palace in 1609. It is a splendid piece of calligraphy.

[Royal MS 18 A xlv, f.2v]

15

16 Robert Herrick
(1591–1674): Elegy on John
Browne.
This formal elegy, dating
from 1619, is the only poem
known to survive in Herrick's
own hand. In writing
'Trinitall halls/Exequies' he
made a simple slip for
'Trinity Hall', his own
college.
[Harley MS 367, f.154]

17 John Milton (1608–1674):
Page from his commonplace
book.
Milton's extracts on 'political
astuteness', taken from
Sidney, Spenser and other
writers, probably belong to a
period after his Italian
journey of 1638–9, and are
accompanied by his
comments written in the
language of the originals. The
final entry was added by a
scribe.
[Add. MS 36354, f.93v]

18 John Milton (1608–1674):
Signature from an autograph-
album.
On 29 November 1651
Milton contributed a
modified quotation from the
Greek New Testament to the
album of a visitor from
Germany. Only the signature,
which shows a momentary
lapse over the Latinised form
of his surname, is autograph.
[Egerton MS 1324, f.85v]

homines ų honores feriendi et evertendi artifex Leicestrius vide de Waltero Essexio
Camd. 264 Elizab. et de duce Norfolcio qui ejus insidiis ad nuptias
cum Mariâ Scotâ inducto. vide et eundem p. 475. Sic alter Essexius
iisdem dolis piit Camd. vol. 2. 176.
Such art us'd the stepdam of Plangus excellently set out by Sidney. l. 2. 356.

Randolphus — Walsingamo ų literas monet ut ille Secretarii, ipse legati technis jam
tandem valediceret et pænitendo divinam misericordiam implora-
rent Camden. vol. 2. p. 27. ipsi tamen in repub. viri integri, et religionis
studiosi habiti quo quis ediscat quanto conscientiæ cum tumultu res
politica tractetur.

The wicked policies of divers deputies ę governours in Ireland see Spenser dialogue of Ireland.

Fides promissorū — Promissorum fidem a principibus exigendam, quatenus eam præstan-
lubrica     tibus expedit. Ita Scotiæ regens professanturium legatis respondit.
Thuanus hist. l. 71. p. 647. cujus dicti vero oare præmisit p. 649.
Imperii aulici arcana, et lubricam fidem populo datam esse
expresse declarant illæ literæ monitoriæ ad Colinium missæ
paulo ante lanienam Parisiensem quibus si paruisset non ita
miserabili occisione cum suis periisset vide Thuan. hist. l. 52.
statim ab initio. p. 805. 806.

Hæc est prudentia seculi istius, quam politicam appellant: utile
quod putant, non dubitant honesto præferre; quod utile judicant, necessarium esse statuant, quod necessarium, licere: Revet. in Bod.
cap. 1.

Ἐν ἀσθενείᾳ τελειοῦμαι

Doctissimo Viro, meoų fautori humanissimo,
D. Christophoro Arnoldo dedi hoc in memo-
riam cum sua virtutis, tum mei erga se studii.
Londini. An: D. 1651. Novem: 19.

           Joannes Miltonius

**19** Sir Thomas Browne (1605–1682): Drafts of passages from *Urne-buriall*.
Difficult as Browne's late-surviving Secretary hand is to decipher, these
passages from Chapter V of his book (1658) have been called the finest piece of
English prose after the Authorised Version of the Bible.
[Sloane MS 1862, f.78v]

**20** 'Percy Folio' of ballads: mid-17th century.
This large anonymous collection, copied in a squareish Secretary hand, is a
principal source for early English balladry. Its margins are filled with
annotations by Bishop Thomas Percy, who rescued it from burning.
[Add. MS 27879, f.94 (top)]

... ... ...
...ll3 Ballads. 1727.
fol. s. p. 508. N°. xv.

94    fol-
188.

God

NB. The Readings in
the margin are taken
from the Scotch Edition
printed at Glasgow
8vo 1747. — wch. is re
-markable for
the wilful Corrup
tions made in
all y
was    Pasa..
...ged, wth concern
the two Nations

Prosper long our noble K
..urless fafty.. all
a woefull hunting onc'd ther was
in Cheviy Chase befall
to driue the Deere wth hound & horne
Erle Peary took the way
the child may rue yt is vnborne
the hunting of y Day

the stout Erle of Northumberland
a Now to god did make
his pleasure in the Scotish woods
3 sommer Days to take
the chefefe harts in Chevy Chase
to kill & bare away
these tydings to Erle Douglas came
in Scotland whare he Lay
who soul Erle Peary sent word
he wold prevent his sport
the English Erle not fearing that
did to the wood resort
wth 1500 bowmen bold
all chosen men of might
who knew full well in tiue of nede
to ayme their shaft arright
the Gallant Greyhound swiftly ran
to Chase the fallow Deere
on Munday they began to hunt
ere Daylight did appeare
& long before high noone the had
a 100 fat buckes slaine
then hauing Dind the Drouyers wente
to rouze the Deere againe

this

20,00

grey honds

when

the

*COMMENTARIES of Heaven.*

WHEREIN

The Mysteries of Felicitie
are *opened:*
and

ALL THINGS
Discovered
to be
Objects of Happiness.

EVRY BEING
Created & Increated
being alphabetically Represented
in the Light
of
GLORY

Therein also .
for ȳ Satisfaction of Atheists, & ȳ Consolation
of Christians, as well as ȳ, Encouragement &
Delight of Divines: & Transcendent Verities
of ȳ Holy Scriptures, celested for ȳ ȳ
Highest Objects of ȳ Christian faith are
in a Clear mirror Exhibited to the
Ey of Reason: in their Realities and
Glory.

21

**21** Thomas Traherne (about 1637–1674): *Commentaries of Heaven.*
Traherne's autograph titlepage – a comparatively rare thing in literary
manuscripts of any period – introduces 400 pages of prose and verse written in
the last two years of his life.
[Add. MS 63054, f.2]

**22** John Dryden (1631–1700): Letter to Lawrence Hyde, Earl of Rochester.
Writing in about August 1683, the Poet Laureate complains to the Lord
Treasurer about his arrears of salary, remarking ''Tis enough for one Age to
have neglected Mr [Abraham] Cowley, and sterv'd Mr [Samuel] Butler'.
[Add. MS 17017, f.49]

My Lord

I know not whether my Lord Sunderland has interceded with your Lord=ship, for half a yeare of my salary: But I have two other Advocates, my extreame wants even almost to arresting, & my ill health which cannot be repaird without immediate retireing into the Country. A quarters allowance is but the Jesuites powder to my disease; the fitt will return a fortnight hence. If I durst I would plead a little merit, & some hazards of my life from the Common Enemyes; my refuseing advantages offerd by them, & neglecting my beneficiall studyes for the Kings service: But I onely thinke I meritt not to sterve. I never applyd my selfe to any Interest contra=ry to your Lordships; and on some occasions, perhaps not known to you, have not been unserviceable to the memory & reputation of My Lord your father. After this, My Lord, my conscience assures me I may write boldly, though I cannot speake to you. I have three Sonns growing to mans estate, I breed them all up to learning beyond my fortune; but they are too hopefull to be neglected though I want. Be pleasd to looke on me with an eye of compassion; some small Employment would render my condition easy. The King is not un=satisfyed of me, the Duke has often promist me his assistance: & Your Lordship is the Conduit through which their favours passe. Either in the Customes, or the Appeales of the Excise, or some other way; meanes cannot be wanting if you please to have the will. Tis enough for one Age to have neglected Mr Cowley, and sterved Mr Butler: but neither of them had the happines to live till your Lordships Ministry. In the meane time be pleasd to give me a gracious and speedy answer to my present request of halfe a yeares pention for my necessityes. I am goeing to write somewhat by his Majestyes command, & cannot stirr into the Country for my health and studies, till I secure my family from want. You have many petitions of this nature, & cannot satisfy all, but I hope from your goodnesse to be made an Exception to your generall rules; because I am, with all sincerity,

          Your Lordships most obedient
              Humble Servant

                                  John Dryden.

*Sam: Johnson*

# The 18th Century

The vastly increased output of the press during the age of reason and enlightenment, and in particular the spread of newspapers and the growth of periodical journalism, finally put an end to the manuscript as a serious means of circulating new information and ideas. Publishers and booksellers (who were often one and the same) were equally ready to disseminate works of literature. As a result, a fair number of such literary manuscripts as have survived originate from the printing-house. Sometimes they have escaped the destruction to which they were normally consigned after setting-up, and sometimes they take the form of authorially-revised proofs, additional passages and so forth. Almost always, unlike the numerous commonplace copies of the previous century, manuscripts are of an essentially private nature: that is, they emanate from the study, if not the wastepaper-basket, of the author – early drafts, perhaps, preserved by chance or sent to friends for amusement or criticism. The habit of friendly intercourse between people of leisure and literary tastes is nowhere better seen than in the mass of fascinating private correspondence that has come down to us from this first great age of letter-writing. The survival of such letters, as of many other kinds of document, owes a great deal to the fashion for autograph-hunting that grew from the private enthusiasm of a few scholarly men in the mid-18th century to become the almost universal hobby of the middle classes during the early decades of the next.

One series of private letters that has achieved the status of a literary work in its own right is that which Jonathan Swift (23) wrote between 1710 and 1713 to his close friend Esther Johnson in Dublin, during his absence in England on a commission from the Irish bishops. It was the dramatist Richard Sheridan who in 1784 printed these, the most personal of Swift's writings, under the title of the *Journal to Stella*, after Swift's pet name for his correspondent. Another great writer whose letters survive in considerable quantities is the poet Alexander Pope, who introduced the notion of 'correctness' into English versification and became as bitter a satirist in verse as his friend Swift was in prose. With true parsimony the backs of letters addressed to Pope between 1712 and 1720 were put to literary use for the drafts of much of his translation of Homer's *Iliad* (24). To aid his imagination, Pope sketched, from Homer's description in Book XIX, the shield forged by Hephaestus for Achilles.

Thomas Gray's famous 'Elegy' (25) survives in three fair-copies made in his own scholarly hand at various times and sent to friends. They must have shared them too freely with others; to forestall an unauthorised edition Gray made arrangements for his friend Horace Walpole in London to oversee the poem's publication. The present manuscript comes the closest of any to the text of the poem as it was brought out on 15 February

1751. Its success was immediate, partly because, as Samuel Johnson remarked, it 'abounds with images which find a mirror in every mind...'.

With Richardson, Fielding, Smollett and Sterne, the mid-18th century witnessed the beginnings of the novel in its modern form. Sterne was forty-seven years of age when he issued, at his own expense, the first instalment of his highly eccentric novel *Tristram Shandy* in 1760. The equally whimsical *Sentimental Journey* (**27**) was inspired by the current taste for travel-books and owed its title to the fashionable interpretation of 'sentimental' as meaning 'full of refined feeling'. The manuscript of Volume I, prepared for the press, was later owned and 'Grangerized', or interspersed with illustrative material, by the most famous of all autograph-collectors, William Upcott (1779–1845), who named his house in Islington 'Autograph Cottage'.

Another of this century's great Irish-born humorists, following Swift and Sterne and preceding Sheridan, was Oliver Goldsmith, who in a short life managed to write minor masterpieces in poetry, drama and the novel, besides much journalistic hack-work. An amusing letter (**26**) of September 1771 includes the earliest-known mention of his famous comedy of manners *She Stoops to Conquer*, first performed at the Covent Garden Theatre on 15 March 1773. It also gives news of Sir Joshua Reynolds and Edmund Burke, co-founders of the literary 'Club' presided over by Dr Samuel Johnson. Many letters and manuscripts of this dominant figure of literary life in mid-18th century London have survived, largely owing no doubt to the enormous esteem in which, as lexicographer, poet, novelist, critic and editor of Shakespeare, he was held during his lifetime. His final major literary undertaking and the maturest product of his critical judgement was his *Lives of the Poets* (1779–1781), from which two sets of very sketchy notes for the 'Life of Pope' (**28**) have come down to us.

To move from Johnson to Burns is to pass from the refined society of the greatest capital-city of its day to a small farm in south-west Scotland, and from orotund Latinate prose to poetry, the finest of which was written in lowland Scots. The well-known song 'The Banks o' Doon' (**29**), which Burns wrote for a collection called *The Scots Musical Museum* in 1792, is one of some 350 that he wrote or revised from traditional lyrics. His bold and angular yet rhythmic handwriting was successfully forged towards the end of the 19th century by Alexander Howland (*alias* 'Antiques') Smith.

William Blake is a transitional figure, a forerunner of the Romantic School and a poetic revolutionary whose greatness as an artist and engraver was not fully appreciated until long after his death. 'The Tyger' (**30**), published in his *Songs of Experience* (1794), is found in draft in a notebook that takes the name 'Rossetti Manuscript' from a later owner, the poet and painter Dante Gabriel Rossetti. In it Blake entered, over the space of a quarter-century, emblems subsequently used in *The Gates of Paradise*, decorations for *The Marriage of Heaven and Hell*, and drafts of prose essays, lyrics and epigrams, together with most of the posthumously-published *Everlasting Gospel*. It is, in short, the classic example of a working-notebook, in which every corner is filled with jottings and drafts.

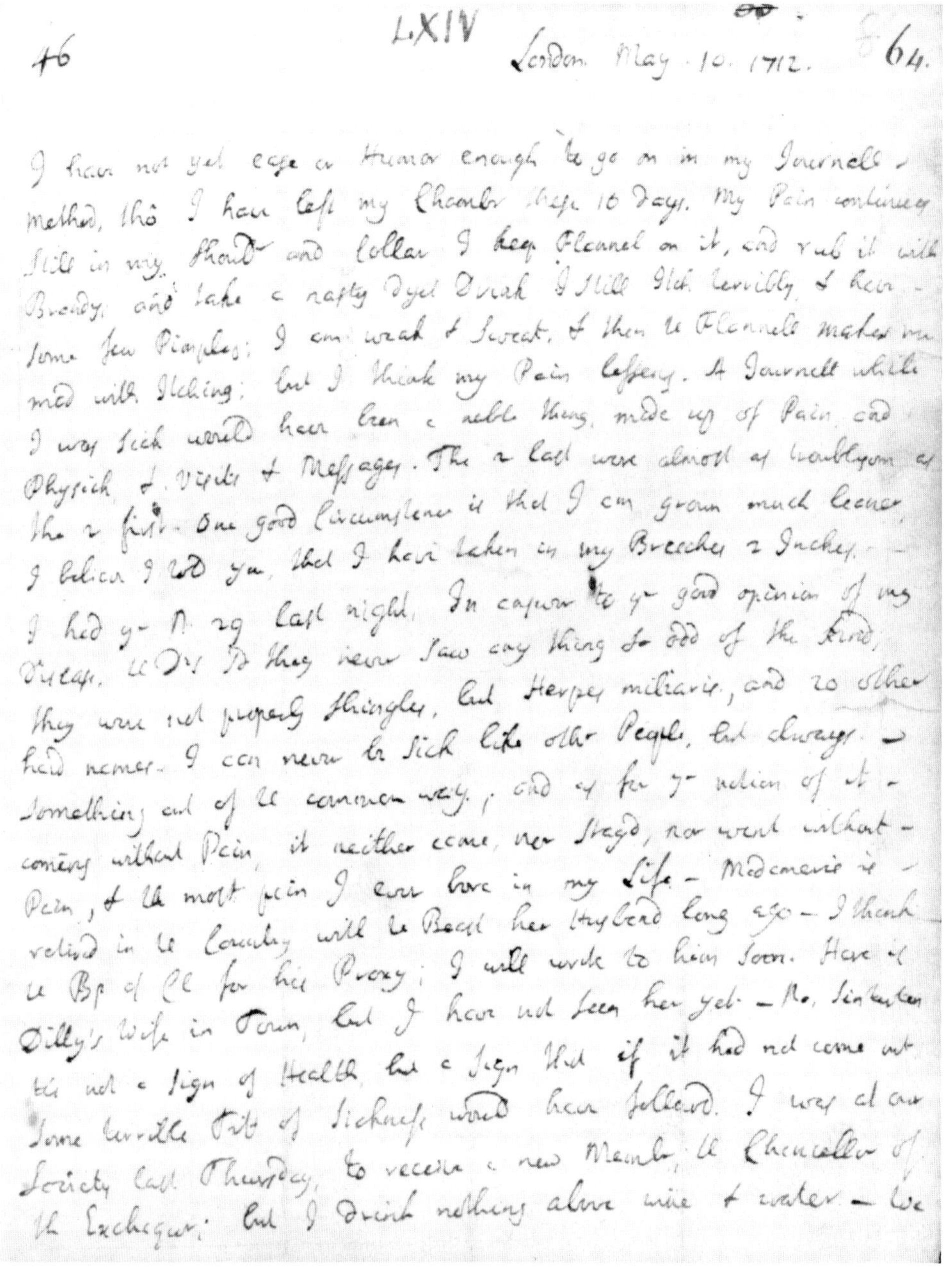

46 LXIV London. May. 10. 1712. 64.

I have not yet ease or Humor enough to go on in my Journall method, tho I have left my Chamber these 10 Days. My Pain continues still in my shouldr and collar I keep Flannel on it, and rub it with Brandy, and take a nasty Dyet Drink I still Itch terribly, & have some few Pimples; I am weak & sweat, & then the Flannell makes me mad with Itching; but I think my Pain lessens. A Journall while I was sick would have been a noble thing, made up of Pain and Physick & visits & Messages. The 2 last were almost as troublesom as the 2 first. One good circumstance is that I am grown much leaner, I believe I told you, that I have taken in my Breeches 2 Inches. I had yr N. 29 last night. In answer to yr good opinion of my Disease, the Drs said they never saw any thing so odd of the kind, they were not properly shingles, but Herpes miliaris, and 20 other hard names. I can never be sick like other People, but always something out of the common way; and as for yr notion of its coming without Pain, it neither came, nor stayd, nor went without Pain, & the most pain I ever bore in my Life. — Medemerie is retired in the Country, will be Beast her Husband long ago — I think the Bp of Cl for his Proxy; I will write to him soon. Here is Dilly's Wife in Town, but I have not seen her yet. — No, Sinkerton 'tis not a sign of Health, but a sign that if it had not come out some terrible Fits of Sickness would have followed. I was at our Society last Thursday, to receive a new Member, the Chancellor of the Exchequer; but I drink nothing above wine & water. — We

**23** Jonathan Swift (1667–1745): Letter to 'Stella'.
Dating from 10 May 1712, this is one of a series of letters that Swift wrote to his friend Esther Johnson during a long absence from his native Dublin between 1710 and 1713.
[Add. MS 4804, f.64]

**24** Alexander Pope (1688–1744): Draft translation of Homer's *Iliad*. Pope's autograph drafts, written between about 1712 and 1720, partly on the backs of letters addressed to him, includes a rough sketch of the shield forged by Hephaestus for Achilles, as described by Homer in Book XIX.

[Add. MS 4808, ff.81v, 82]

Elegy, written in a Country-Churchyard.

The Curfew tolls the Knell of parting Day,
The lowing Herd wind slowly o'er the Lea,
The Ploughman homeward plods his weary Way,
And leaves the World to Darkness & to me.
Now fades the glimm'ring Landscape on the Sight,
And all the Air a solemn Stillness holds;
Save where the Beetle wheels his droning Flight,
Or drowsy Tinklings lull the distant Folds.
Save that from yonder ivy-mantled Tower
The mopeing Owl does to the Moon complain
Of such, as wand'ring near her secret Bower
Molest her ancient solitary Reign.
Beneath those rugged Elms, that Yewtree's Shade,
Where heaves the Turf in many a mould'ring Heap,
Each in his narrow Cell for ever laid,
The rude Forefathers of the Hamlet sleep.
The breezy Call of incense-breathing Morn,
The Swallow twitt'ring from the straw-built Shed,
The Cock's shrill Clarion, & the ecchoing Horn,
No more shall rouse them from their lowly Bed.
For them no more the blazing Hearth shall burn,
Or busy Houswife ply her evening Care;
No Children run to lisp their Sire's Return,
Nor climb his Knees the envied Kiss to share.
Oft did the Harvest to their Sickle yield,
Their Furrow oft the stubborn Glebe has broke;
How jocund did they drive their Team a-field!
How bow'd the Woods beneath their sturdy Stroke!
Let not Ambition mock their useful Toil,
Their homely Joys & Destiny obscure;
Nor Grandeur hear with a disdainful Smile
The short & simple Annals of the Poor.
The Boast of Heraldry, the Pomp of Power,
And all that Beauty, all that Wealth e'er gave,
Awaits alike th' inevitable Hour.
The Paths of Glory lead but to the Grave.
Forgive, ye Proud, th' involuntary Fault,
If Memory to these no Trophies raise,
Where thro' the long-drawn Isle & fretted Vault
The pealing Anthem swells the Note of Praise.
Can storied Urn or animated Bust
Back to its Mansion call the fleeting Breath?
Can Honour's Voice provoke the silent Dust,
Or Flatt'ry sooth the dull cold Ear of Death?

25

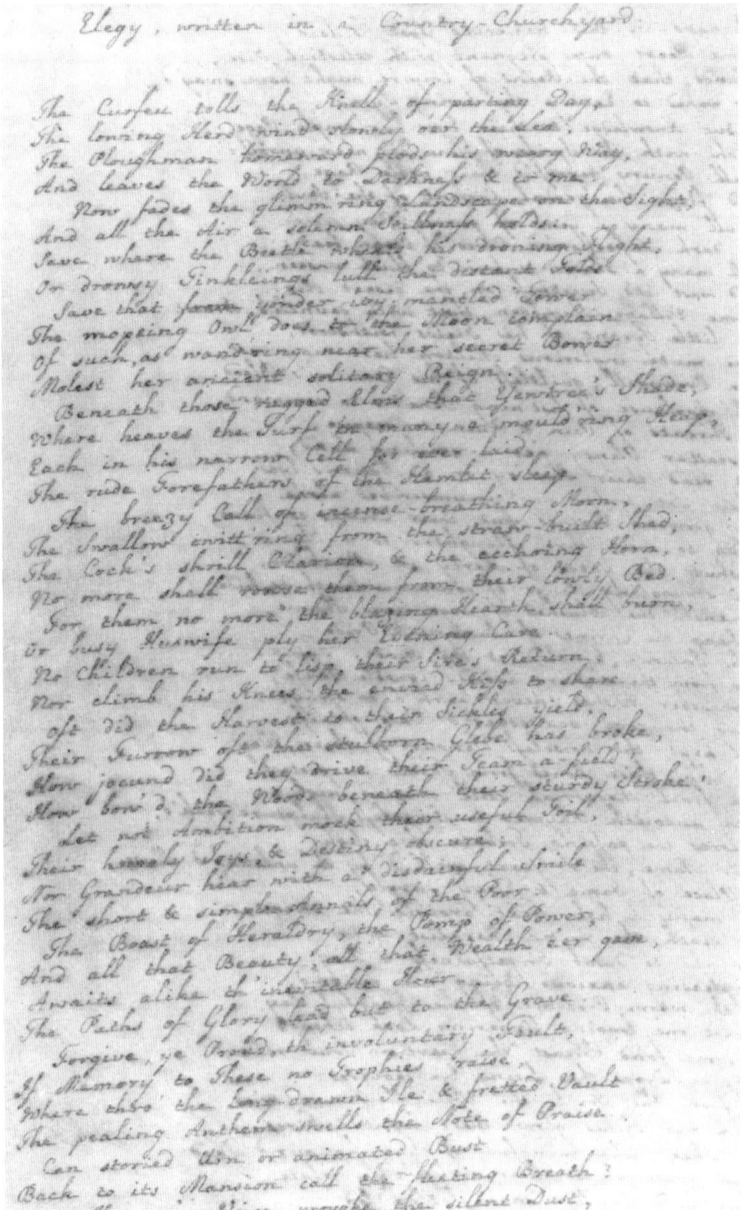

**25** Thomas Gray (1716–1771): 'Elegy Written in a Country Churchyard'. Gray's autograph fair copy of his famous poem, dateable to late 1750, is a fair specimen of his sloping deliberate hand, and a frightening example of how the iron-based ink used at the time can eat through paper.
[Egerton MS 2400, f.45]

**26** Oliver Goldsmith (about 1630–1774): Letter to Bennet Langton.
In this amusing letter of 7 September 1771 Goldsmith complains to a member of Dr Johnson's literary circle of the treatment meted out by critics to his newly-published *Abridgement of the History of England*.
[Add. MS 42515, f.49v]

**27** Laurence Sterne (1713–1768): *A Sentimental Journey through France and Italy*.
Transcribed in about 1767–1768, this fair copy, which was later interleaved with illustrations, extends only as far as the first volume of the published work.
[Egerton MS 1610, ff.127v, 128]

is still as loud as ever. I have published or Davis has published for me an abridgement of the History of England for which I have been a good deal abused in the news papers for betraying the liberties of the people. God knows I had no thoughts for or against liberty in my head. My whole aim being to make up a book of a decent size that as 'Squire Richard says would do no harm to nobody. However they set me down as an arrant Tory and consequently no honest man. When you come to look at any part of it you'l say that I am a sauna Whig. God bless you, and with my most respectful compliments to her Ladyship I remain dear Sir

your most affectionate
humble servant

Oliver Goldsmith.

Gamble
Brick Court
Sept. 7th 1771.

101

### The Bidet.

THE BIDET.

Having settled all these little matters, I got into my post chaise with more ease than ever I got into a post chaise in my life; and La Fleur having got one large jack boot on the far side of a little Bidet, and another on this (for I count nothing of his legs) — he canter'd away before me as happy and as perpendicular as a prince —

—— but what is happiness! what is grandeur in this painted scene of life! a dead ass, before we had got a league, put a sudden stop to La Fleur's career —— his Bidet would not pass by

## Pope (2)

Nothing occasional. no haste. no rivals. no compulsion.

Practised only one form of verse.
facility from use.

Emulated former pieces. Coopers hill - Drydens Ode.

Affected to disdain Flattery - but lap[-]ses in his Selection of Patrons. Cobham, Burlington, Bolingbroke.

Argyle Bot.

Scholar Dobson

Poem long delayed

Satire and praise [Cata] alluding to some dirty poet.

He had always some poetical plans in his head. Pints of Wine

Gravitations on established original

Perugue

Rhyme often worse. Echo to the sense

Would not compromise himself too much

Felicities of Language - Walsh.

[Luxury] of Language

Prudent and Frugal.

28 Dr Samuel Johnson (1709–1784): Notes for his *Life of Pope*.
These memoranda for the longest and last-written of the *Lives of the Poets* belong to about 1780–1781. Johnson's handwriting is as strongly individual as his critical views and his prose-style.
[Add. MS 5994, f. 159]

29 Robert Burns (1759–1796): 'The Banks o' Doon'.
Burns's popular song-lyric dates, in its present form, from about 1791–1792, and was written to fit the well-known tune called 'The Caledonian Hunt's Delight'.
[Add. MS 22307, f.97]

28

93. The Banks o' Doon

Ye banks & braes, o' bonie Doon, ~~Caledonian Hunt's delight~~

How can ye bloom sae fresh & fair;

How can ye chant, ye little birds,

And I sae weary fu' o' care!

Thou'll break my heart, thou warbling bird,

That wantons thro' the flowering thorn!

Thou minds me o' departed joys,

Departed, never to return.—

Oft hae I rov'd by bonie Doon

To see the rose & woodbine twine;

And ilka bird sang o' its Luve,

And fondly sae did I o' mine.—

Wi' lightsome heart I pu'd a rose,

Fu' sweet upon its thorny tree;

And my fause Luver staw my rose,

But, ah! he left the thorn wi' me.—

29

**30** William Blake (1757–1827): Poem and sketch of 'The Tyger'. In this autograph draft, dating from some time before 1794, Blake has dispensed entirely with punctuation. The sketch of a tiger in the same 'Rossetti Manuscript' was made to illustrate a ballad written by a contemporary.

[Add. MS 49460, ff.56 and 3v (details)]

# The 19th Century

Most of the outstanding writers of this astonishingly prolific century, which witnessed the rise of both the Romantic movement and the English novel (in which, as Jane Austen wrote, 'the greatest powers of the mind are displayed') are represented in the British Library's collections.

The first great achievements in poetry of the Romantic movement were the product of the deep friendship between Wordsworth and Coleridge. Coleridge's *Poems on Various Subjects* (**33**) had already appeared in a second edition when his publisher Joseph Cottle agreed to bring out the collection of *Lyrical Ballads* (1798) which he and Wordsworth had written together, largely during the period of intense creativity when they were living close to each other in Somerset. In a famous passage from the *Preface* to the second edition (1800), Wordsworth described poetry as 'the spontaneous overflow of powerful feelings' which 'takes its origin from emotion recollected in tranquillity'. Seven years later Coleridge took a hand in preparing for the press his friend's *Poems, in Two Volumes.* Wordsworth's own share in the copying of the printer's manuscript (**31**) was limited: the bulk of the work was undertaken by a small band of devoted helpers – his sister Dorothy (**32**), wife Mary and sister-in-law Sara Hutchinson. It was not until after the two poets had quarrelled irrevocably, however, that Coleridge, at the suggestion of Lord Byron, printed the fragment of 'Kubla Khan' (**34**) which he claimed to have composed during an opium-dream in 1797.

The second generation of English Romantics – Byron, Shelley and Keats – are almost as famous for their dramatic life stories as for their poetry. They lived intensely, travelled widely and died young – Byron of fever while fighting for the Greeks at Missolonghi, Shelley by drowning in the bay of Lerici and Keats of consumption in Rome. Byron's poetry, although widely condemned on moral grounds and often fiercely attacked by critics, was immensely popular in England and abroad and greatly influenced other poets of the Romantic movement; 'Don Juan' (**38**) was much admired by Goethe and the 'Byronic hero' played an important part in shaping the imagination of the young Brontës. The sonnet by Shelley illustrated here (**37**), was written during the summer of 1816, which he spent on Lake Geneva with Byron.

Keats, whose death is mourned in Shelley's famous poem 'Adonais' (1821), has always been regarded as one of the most brilliant of all the

*3*

O Nightingale! thou surely art
A Creature of a fiery heart —
These notes of thine they pierce, and pierce;
Tumultuous harmony and fierce!
Thou sing'st as if the God of wine
Had help'd thee to a Valentine;
A song in mockery and despite
Of shades, and dews, and silent Night,
And steady bliss, and all the Loves
Now sleeping in these peaceful groves!

Romantics. His letters, first published in 1848, are, in T. S. Eliot's words, 'certainly the most notable and most important ever written by any English poet'. Many contain valuable comments on his poetry and the processes of its composition, interspersed with gossip, and affectionate and lively humour (39).

It is interesting to compare the working methods of two 19th-century novelists represented in the Library's collections. Jane Austen, a parson's daughter, was connected with the landed and professional classes, and it is to their world that she confined herself in her novels, writing to a niece that '3 or 4 families in a country village is the very thing to work on' and to a nephew of 'the little bit (two Inches wide) of Ivory on which I work with so fine a brush, as produces little effect after much labour'. Her novels were written in the intervals of a busy family life, the last three (*Mansfield Park*, *Emma* and *Persuasion*, of which the Library possesses a draft of the final chapter) in the parlour of her mother's cottage at Chawton, in Hampshire. In a 'Biographical Notice' to *Northanger Abbey*, posthumously published in 1818, her brother Henry wrote that 'Though in composition she was equally rapid and correct, yet an invincible distrust of her own judgement induced her to withold her books from the public, till time and many perusals had satisfied her that the charm of recent composition was dissolved.' The Juvenilia, written in her teens, are already witty and elegantly expressed, as the parody 'History of England' (35) reveals.

Dickens, the most prolific and dramatic of 19th-century novelists, had none of Jane Austen's scruples. Like Thackeray (41, 42) he had a wife and family to support, and he craved the trappings, rewards and excitement of

31 William Wordsworth (1770–1850): 'O Nightingale! thou surely art'.
This autograph fair-copy of a poem composed about February 1807 comes from the manuscript for *Poems, in Two Volumes* (1807), which was transcribed by members of the Wordsworth household over a six-month period and sent to the publisher in packets.
[Add. MS 47864, f.58v (detail)]

fame. The entries in his diary for the fortnight before he finished *Nicholas Nickleby* (44) consist mostly of the single word 'Work'. On Friday 20 September 1839 he wrote: 'Finished Nickleby this day at 2 o'Clock... Thank God that I have lived to get through it happily'. Like *Pickwick Papers* (the manuscript of part of which is also owned by the Library), which preceded it, it was published in monthly instalments; Dickens was never very far ahead of publication and had little time for revision until his works were republished in later editions.

The Library is fortunate in its possession of a splendid collection of Brontë material, including juvenilia now in the Ashley collection of manuscripts formed by Thomas Wise. The children's imaginary worlds of Gondal (created by Emily and Anne) and Angria (created by Charlotte and Branwell) were chronicled in extraordinarily elaborate and accomplished prose tales and poems, written out in tiny notebooks in a special 'printing' hand. Emily, the most gifted poet of the four, is now accepted as one of the most original voices of the century, celebrated for her lyrical and visionary poems (48). Charlotte completed her second novel, *Jane Eyre*, in 1847 (47). The story of passionate love checked by moral scruples and beset by apparently insurmountable difficulties achieved immediate success; Thackeray 'lost a whole day in reading it' and it remains one of the most widely read of all English novels.

Perhaps the most famous of all the Library's 19th-century manuscripts, however, is *Alice's Adventures under Ground* (50), written and illustrated for the ten-year-old Alice Liddell by Charles Lutwidge Dodgson, a shy mathematics don at Christ Church, Oxford. As an old lady, widowed and owing substantial death duties, Alice was compelled to sell her treasured manuscript. It was bought by a private collector in the United States, after whose death a group of Americans, led by the Librarian of Congress, repurchased it and offered it as a gift to the British people in recognition of their courage during the Second World War. It was presented to the British Museum in 1948 and has been on display ever since.

32 Dorothy Wordsworth (1771–1855): Fair copy of her brother's poem 'The Rainbow'.
Many of the copies in Dorothy's hand that were used in the manuscript of the 1807 *Poems* were taken from a collection transcribed the previous Spring. This one was sent off attached by sewing-thread to the foot of 'O Nightingale' (31).
[Add. MS 47864, f.59v]

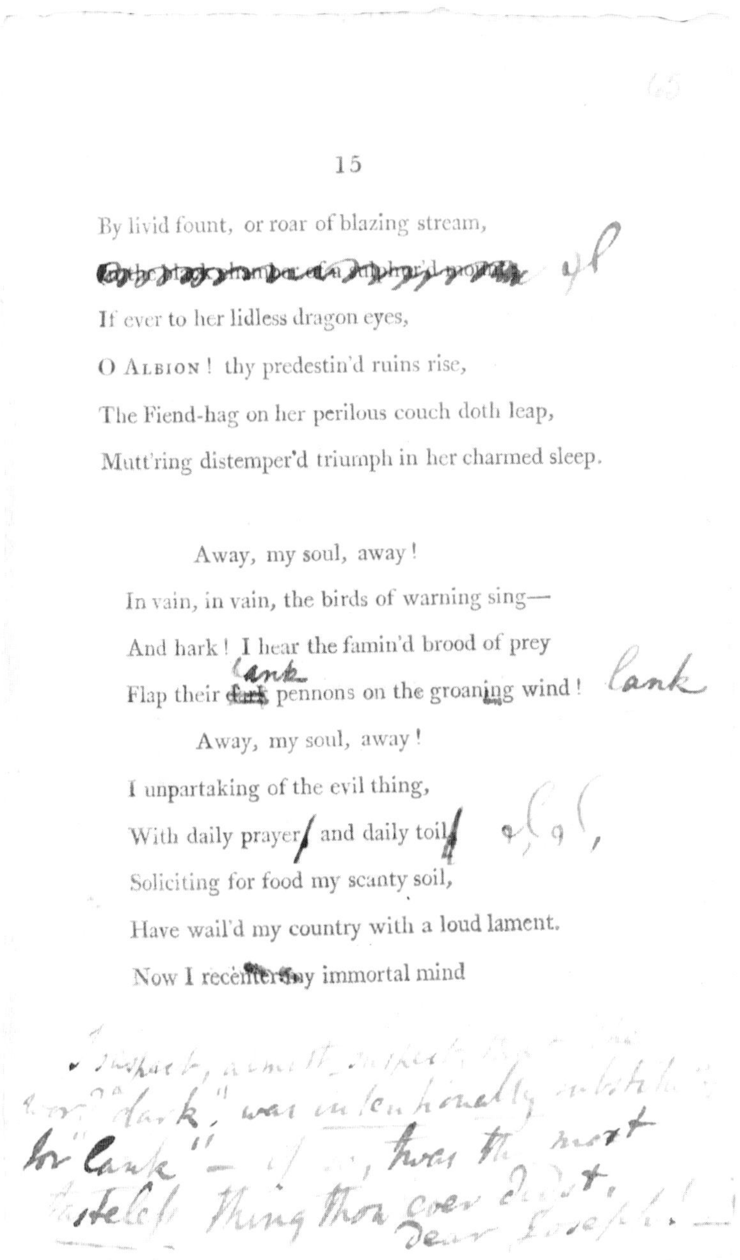

15

By livid fount, or roar of blazing stream,

~~Or o'er black hamlet on the murd'rous gloom,~~ *yf*

If ever to her lidless dragon eyes,

O ALBION ! thy predestin'd ruins rise,

The Fiend-hag on her perilous couch doth leap,

Mutt'ring distemper'd triumph in her charmed sleep.


Away, my soul, away !

In vain, in vain, the birds of warning sing—

And hark ! I hear the famin'd brood of prey

Flap their ~~dark~~ *lank* pennons on the groaning wind !  *lank*

Away, my soul, away !

I unpartaking of the evil thing,

With daily prayer/ and daily toil/  *q, q (,*

Soliciting for food my scanty soil,

Have wail'd my country with a loud lament.

Now I recenter my immortal mind

*[handwritten annotation, partly illegible]*
*... for "dark," was intentionally ... for "lank" — ... ... twas the most ... thing thou ever didst, dear Joseph!*

33

33 Samuel Taylor Coleridge (1772–1834): Corrected proofs of his 'Ode on the Departing Year'.
The characteristic comments added by the author on proofs of his *Poems on Various Subjects* (1797) were addressed to their publisher Joseph Cottle, who also brought out the *Lyrical Ballads* of 1798.
[Ashley MS 408, f.65]

34 Samuel Taylor Coleridge (1772–1834): 'Kubla Khan'.
The only-known manuscript of Coleridge's most famous poem is a fair copy made for an admirer at sometime between 1797 and 1816. It differs in several respects from the version published in the latter year at the request of Lord Byron.
[Add. MS 50847, f.1v]

In a vision once I saw:
It was an Abyssinian Maid,
And on her Dulcimer she play'd
Singing of Mount Amara.
Could I revive within me
Her Symphony & Song,
To such a deep Delight 'twould win me,
That with Music loud and long
I would build that Dome in Air,
That sunny Dome! those Caves of Ice!
And all, who heard, should see them there,
And all should cry, Beware! Beware!
His flashing Eyes! his floating Hair!
Weave a circle round him thrice,
And close your Eyes in holy Dread.
For He on Honey-dew hath fed
And drank the Milk of Paradise.————

This fragment with a good deal more, not
recoverable, composed, in a sort of Reverie brought
on by two grains of Opium, taken to check a
dysentery, at a Farm House between Porlock &
Linton, a quarter of a mile from Culbone Church,
in the fall of the year, 1797.————

           S. T. Coleridge

34

*disgrace to humanity, that pest of society, Eliza-beth. Many were the people who fell Martyrs to the protestant Religion during her reign; I suppose not fewer than a dozen. She married Philip King of Spain who in her Sister's reign for famous for building Armadas. She died without issue, & then the dreadful moment came in which the destroyer of all comfort, the deceitful Betrayer of trust reposed in her, & the Murderess of her Cousin succeeded to the Throne. —*

*Elizabeth*

**35** Jane Austen (1775–1817): 'The History of England'.
This account, 'by a partial, prejudiced and ignorant historian', was written
when Jane Austen was fifteen, and illustrated with portraits drawn by her sister
Cassandra. It makes fun of popular abridgements relying more upon
imagination than research. (*Illustrated in colour on p. 80.*)
[Add. MS 59874, f.171]

**36** Charles Lamb (1775–1834): Letter to Bernard Barton.
Lamb was a prolific and entertaining correspondent. This letter, written in 1823
towards the close of his thirty-three years as a clerk with the East India
Company, dramatically describes the miseries of a life dependent upon 'book-
drudgery' and gives thanks that he has chosen to earn his livelihood by other
means. 'Keep to your Bank' he advises his friend, 'and the Bank will keep you.'
[Add. MS 35256, f.7]

"Throw yourself on the world without any rational plan of support beyond what the chance employ of Booksellers would afford you"!!!

Throw yourself rather, my dear Sir, from the steep Tarpeian rock slap-dash headlong upon iron spikes. If you had but five consolatory minutes between the desk and the bed, make much of them, and live a century in them, rather than turn slave to the Booksellers. They are Turks and Tartars, when they have poor Authors at their beck. Hitherto you have been at arms' length from them. Come not within their grasp. I have known many authors for bread, some repining, others envying the blessed security of a Counting House, all agreeing they had rather have been Taylors, Weavers, what not? rather than the things they were. I have known some starved, some to go mad, one dear friend literally dying in a workhouse. You know not what

To Laughter

Thy friends were never mine thou heartless
                    fiend:
Silence and solitude & calm & storm
Hope, before whose veiled shrine all
                    spirits bend
In worship, & the rainbow vested form
Of conscience, that within thy hollow heart
Can find no throne—the love of such great
                    powers
Which hast requited mine in many hours
Of loneliness, thou ne'er hast felt; depart!
Thou canst not bear the moon's great eye, thou
                    fearest
A fair child clothed in smiles—aught that is high
Or good or beautiful.— Thy voice is deadest
To those who mock at truth & Innocence;
I now alone, weep without shame to see
How many broken hearts lie bare to thee.

**37** Percy Bysshe Shelley (1792–1822): 'To Laughter'.
Among the collection of letters, bills, betting slips and other memorabilia
belonging to Byron's friend Scrope Davies, discovered in a London bank vault
in 1976, was a notebook containing two hitherto unknown sonnets by Shelley.
This, the second sonnet, transcribed by Shelley's wife Mary in 1816, looks
forward to one of his greatest lyrics, 'When the lamp is shattered', written six
years later.
[Loan 70, volume 8, f.1v]

**38** George Gordon, Lord Byron (1788–1824): 'Don Juan'.

Byron began 'Don Juan', his longest and most famous poem, in 1818; the first two cantos were published, anonymously, by John Murray in the following year and immediately denounced as 'filthy and impious' by *Blackwood's Magazine*. This is a heavily altered draft of the fifteenth stanza of the 'Dedication' to the poem.

[Ashley MS B.4732, f.128]

**39** John Keats (1795–1821): Letter to his brother Tom.
In the summer of 1818, when he was touring Scotland with a friend, Keats
wrote a series of long journal letters to his youngest brother, gravely ill with
consumption at home in Hampstead. Here he has copied out a sonnet, 'To
Ailsa Rock', which captures his excited delight in scenery of a starkness and
grandeur he had never encountered before.
[Add. MS 45510, f.1v]

**40** Elizabeth Barret Browning (1806–1861): 'Sonnets from the Portuguese'.
The title of this sonnet sequence, which describes the gradual flowering of the
invalid Elizabeth Barrett's love for Robert Browning, is a secret reference to his
nickname for her, 'the Portuguese', derived from one of her poems. This last
sonnet is dated September 1846, the month of the couple's elopement to Italy:
the words '*Married – September 12th*' have been added by Elizabeth beneath it.
[Add. Ms 43487, f.50]

## XLIV

Belovèd, thou hast brought me many flowers
Plucked in the garden, all the summer through,
And winter; and it seemed as if they grew
In this close room, nor missed the sun or showers.
So, in the like name of that love of ours,
Take back these thoughts which here, unfolded, too,
And which on warm or cold days I withdrew
From my heart's ground — (indeed those beds o'bowers
Be overgrown with bitter weeds & rue
And wait thy weeding; yet here's eglantine —
here's ivy! —
— take them, as I used to do.
Thy flowers, and keep them where they shall not pine!
Instruct thine eyes to keep their colours true,
And tell thy soul, their roots are left in mine —

oo Wimpole Street
1846, Sept.

married — September 12th.
1846 —

40

Though I have not written to my
dearest Nanny, since I came away,
I think about her many many times;
and pray God for her and Baby
and to make them both well and good.
You will be well I hope in the spring
when we will take a house by the sea-
-side, and you can go into the fields
and pick flowers, as you used to do
at Margate : before Mamma was ill
and when Baby was only a little child in
arms. Please God, Mamma n will
be made well one day too. How glad
I shall be to see all my darlings well
again : and there is somebody else

41 William Makepeace
Thackeray (1811–1863):
Letter to his daughters Anne
and Harriet.
In 1840 Thackeray's wife
Isabella suffered a severe
mental breakdown. His two
small daughters were sent to
live with their grandmother
in Paris, while he strove to
make his name as a writer in
London. This letter was sent
to them in 1842; Anne's
attempt to copy the first word
can be seen beneath it.
[Add. MS 46892, f.123]

**42** William Makepeace Thackeray (1811–1863): Letter to his mother. Written on the inside of this envelope, which contained letters from his two daughters to their grandmother in Paris, dated 30 November 1853, is a postscript from Thackeray. The three were at Marseilles, about to embark on a steamer for Genoa.

[Add. MS 46893, f.147]

**43** Alfred, Lord Tennyson (1809–1892): 'Tears, idle Tears'. Tennyson presented this manuscript of a well-known lyric from *The Princess* (published in 1847) to his friend Francis Turner Palgrave in 1854. The first line has been altered from the less haunting 'Ah foolish tears...'.

[Add. MS 45741, f.281]

to rebell you , and a garnet ring belonging to my
ma , and having not been apprehended by the
constables it is supposed to have been
took up by some stage - coach. They
beg that if he comes to you the ring
may be returned and that you will let the
thief and assassin go , as if prose-
cuted him he would only be transported and
if he is let go he is sure to be hung in time
which will save us trouble and be much more
satisfactory . Hoping to hear from
you when convenient

          " I remain
               " Yours and other
                    " Fanny Squeers.

P.S. I pity his ignorance and despise him .

     A profound silence succeeded to the reading
of this choice epistle during which Newman Noggs
as he folded it up gazed with a kind of
grotesque pity at the boy of desperate character
therein referred to, who , having no more
distinct perception of the matter in hand
than that he had been the unfortunate
cause of heaping trouble and falsehood
upon Nicholas sat mute and dispirited with a

**44** Charles Dickens (1812–1870): *Nicholas Nickleby.*
Dickens worked on this immensely popular novel, which was published in monthly parts, during 1838 and 1839. The page shown here contains part of Fanny Squeers's ludicrously indignant letter describing the events immediately preceding Nicholas's escape from Dotheboys' Hall with the 'boy of desperate character', Smike.
[Add. MS 57483, f.10]

**45** Edward Lear (1812–1888): 'How pleasant to know Mr Lear!'
Lear sent this dedication copy of a poem first published in *Nonsense Songs and Stories* (1895) to the daughter of a friend. In the published version the runcible hat ceased to be brown, the jujubes became pancakes and the spelling of 'pillgrimage', a pun on the poet's chronic ill-health, was 'corrected', probably by the printer.
[Add. MS 61891 P]

Chap I.

1.

In writing these pages, which for the want of a better name I shall be fain to call the autobiography of so insignificant a person as myself, it will not be so much my intention to speak of the little details of my private life, as of what I, and perhaps others round me, have done in literature, of my failures and successes such as they have been, and their causes, and of the opening which a literary career offers to men & women for the earning of their bread. And yet the garrulity of old age, and the aptitude of a man's mind to recur to the passages of his own life, will I know tempt me to say something of myself; — nor without doing so should I know how to throw my matter into any recognised and intelligible form. That I, or any man, should tell everything of himself, I hold to be impossible. Who could endure to own the doing of a mean thing? Who is there that has done none? But this I protest; — that nothing that I say shall be untrue. I will set down naught in malice; nor will I give to myself, or others, honour which I do not believe to have been fairly won.

My boyhood was I think as unhappy as that of a young gentleman could well be, my misfortune arising from a mixture of poverty and gentle standing on the part of my father, and from an utter want on my own part of that juvenile manhood which enables some boys to hold up their heads even among the distresses which such a position is sure to produce.

I was born in 1815, in Keppel Street Russell Square, and while a baby was carried down to Harrow where

**46** Anthony Trollope (1815–1882): *Autobiography.*
This memoir was completed in 1876 and entrusted to Trollope's son Henry, with the request that it should 'be published after my death, and be edited by you'. When the first edition appeared in 1883, some critics expressed disappointment at its matter-of-fact, deliberately unsensational tone.
[Add. Ms 42856, f.3]

Profound silence fell when he had uttered that word with deep
but low intonation. Presently Mr Wood said:

"I cannot proceed without some investigation into what has
been asserted, and evidence of its truth or falsehood."

"The ceremony is quite broken off;" subjoined the voice behind us "I am in a condition to prove my allegation - an insuperable impediment to this marriage exists."

Mr Rochester heard but heeded not - he stood stubborn and rigid,
making no movement but to possess himself of my hand - what
a hot and strong grasp he had - and how like quarried marble
was his pale, firm, massive front at this moment! - how his
eyes shone, still - watchful and yet wild beneath - !

Mr Wood seemed at a loss: "What is the nature of the
impediment?" he asked "Perhaps it may be got over - explained
away?"

"Hardly;" was the answer "I have called it insuperable and
I speak advisedly." The speaker came forwards and leant on the
rails: he continued, uttering each word distinctly, calmly, steadily,
but not loudly "It simply consists in the existence of a previous
marriage: Mr Rochester has a wife now living."

My nerves vibrated to these ~~soft~~ low-spoken ~~whispered~~ words as they had
never vibrated to thunder - my blood felt their subtle vio-
lence as it had never felt ~~from or~~ frost or fire - but I was collected and in no danger of swooning. I looked at Mr Rochester,
I made him look at me - his whole face was colourless rock,

**47** Charlotte Bronte: (1816–1855): *Jane Eyre.*
In August 1847 Charlotte Bronte sent this fair copy of her second novel to
Smith, Elder and Co., the only publishing house to write her an encouraging
letter about her earlier work, *The Professor.* It is remarkably neat, with
relatively few corrections: a beautiful example of what her biographer, Mrs
Gaskell, described as her 'clear, legible, delicate traced writing'.
[Add. MS 43475, f.237]

Now, when alone, do my thoughts no longer hover
Over the mountains on Angora's shore;
Resting their wings where heath and fern-leaves cover
That noble heart for ever, ever more?

Cold in the earth, and fifteen wild Decembers
From those brown hills have melted into spring –
Faithful indeed is the spirit that remembers
After such years of change and suffering!

Sweet Love of youth, forgive if I forget thee
While the world's tide is bearing me along
Sterner desires and darker hopes beset me
Hopes which obscure but cannot do thee wrong –

No other sun has lightened up my heaven;
No other star has ever shone for me
All my life's bliss from thy dear life was given –
All my life's bliss is in the grave with thee

But when the days of golden dreams had perished
And even Despair was powerless to destroy
Then did I learn how existence could be cherished
Strengthened and fed without the aid of joy

Then did I check the tears of useless passion,
Weaned my young soul from yearning after thine;
Sternly denied its burning wish to hasten
Down to that tomb already more than mine!

And even yet, I dare not let it languish,
Dare not indulge in Memory's rapturous pain
Once drinking deep of that divinest anguish
How could I seek the empty world again?

May 17th 1945

H.A. and A.S.

In the same place, when Nature wore
The same celestial glow;
I'm sure I've seen these forms before
But many springs ago;

**48** Emily Brontë (1818–1848): *Gondal Poems.*

Gondal, an imaginary world created by Emily Brontë and her sister Anne, provided the setting for many of Emily's poems; the initials and names attached to them represent characters in the Gondal epic, of which nothing in prose remains. This notebook is written in Emily's minute 'printing' hand.

[Add. MS 43483, f.27]

**49** George Eliot (Mary Ann Evans) (1819–1880): *Middlemarch.* Virginia Woolf described this, George Eliot's masterpiece, as 'one of the few English novels written for grown-up people'. It was published in instalments in 1871–2; this is the copy sent to the printer, afterwards presented by the author to her beloved companion, George Henry Lewes.

[Add. MS 34034, f.151]

" Follows here the strict receipt
For that sauce to dainty meat,
Called Idleness, which many eat
By preference, & call it sweet :
    First watch for morsels, like a hound,
    Mix well with buffets, stir them round
    With good thick oil of flatteries
    And froth with mean self-lauding lies.
    Hot serve : the vessels you must choose
To keep it in are dead men's shoes."

Mr. Bulstrode's consultation of "Harriet" seemed to have had the effect desired by Mr. Vincy, for early the next morning a letter came which Fred could carry to his uncle Featherstone as the required testimony.

The old gentleman was staying in bed on account of the cold weather, & as Mary Garth was not to be seen in the sitting room Fred went upstairs immediately & presented the letter to his uncle, who, propped up comfortably on a bed-rest, was not less able than usual to enjoy his consciousness of wisdom in distrusting & frustrating mankind. He put on his spectacles to read the letter, pursing up his lips & drawing down their corners.

" Under the circumstances I will not decline to state my conviction — tchah! what fine words the fellow puts! He's as fine as an auctioneer — that your son Frederic has not obtained any advance of money on bequests of Mr Featherstone — promised? who said I had ever promised? I promise nothing — I shall make codicils as long as I like — that considering the nature of such a proceeding, it is unreasonable to presume that a young man of sense & character would attempt it

"The Queen of Hearts she made some tarts
   All on a summer day:
The Knave of Hearts he stole those tarts,
   And took them quite away!"

"Now for the evidence," said the King, "and then the sentence."

"No!" said the Queen, "first the sentence, and then the evidence!"

"Nonsense!" cried Alice, so loudly that everybody jumped, "the idea of having the sentence first!"

"Hold your tongue!" said the Queen.

"I won't!" said Alice, "you're nothing but a pack of cards! Who cares for you?"

At this the whole pack rose up into the air, and came flying down upon her: she gave a little scream of fright, and tried to beat them off, and found herself lying on the bank, with her head in the lap of her sister, who was gently brushing away some leaves that had fluttered down from the trees on to her face.

After this disclosure ~~Tess~~ Tess nourished no further ~~foolish~~ thought
that there ~~lurked any grave &~~ deliberate ~~meaning~~ import in Clare's attentions
~~to~~ her. It was a passing summer love of her face, for love's
own temporary sake – nothing more. ~~But~~ And the thorny crown of
this sad ~~thought~~ conclusion was that she whom he really did prefer in ~~this~~ 50
passing, way, ~~a to the rest,~~ she who knew herself to be more impassioned in
nature, ~~more clever~~ cleverer, more beautiful than they, was in the eyes
of society far less worthy ~~&~~ of him than the ~~meanest~~ meaner ones whom he
ignored.

## Chapter XXIII

Amid the oozing fatness & warm ferments of ~~the~~ Frome Vale, at a
season when the rush of juices (~~below~~ & the hiss of fertilization) could almost
be heard, it was impossible that the most fanciful love should not grow
passionate. The ~~forward~~ ready hearts existing there were impregnated by
their ~~environment; the slumberous enervating air weighed upon~~
surroundings.

July passed over their heads, & the Thermidorean weather
which came in its train seemed ~~determined~~ an effort on the part of Nature to match the state
of ~~feminine~~ hearts at Talbothays Dairy. The air of the place,
so fresh in the Spring, ~~was slumberous~~ & early summer. was stagnant & enervating now.
Its heavy scents weighed upon them, ~~though~~ & Ethiopic scorchings browned
the upper slopes of the ~~grass~~ pastures, but there was still bright green where the watercourses
purled. ~~This~~ And as Clare ~~the young people~~ was oppressed by the outward heats
~~so~~ so was he burdened inwardly by a ~~gushing~~ waxing fervour of passion
~~no less than inward~~ ~~for the~~ for the
~~to tempt Clare. for the seductive Tess~~ soft & silent Tess.

*(left margin:)* & at mid-day the landscape seemed, lying in a swoon.

notebooks is their scrapbook-like quality: Sassoon has pasted in, or loosely inserted, photographs of himself, his family and friends; old maps of hunt-meets; cuttings from *Country Life* and *Horse and Hound*; and obituaries of sporting acquaintances described in the course of the story. Faced with such a manuscript, Larkin's 'two kinds of value . . . the magical . . . and the meaningful' merge into one.

29. A bath room, with a couple of bath gowns hanging up. Mrs Pearce comes in, followed by Eliza.

ELIZA. Good! whats this? Is this where you wash the clothes? Funny sort of copper, I call it.

MRS PEARCE. It is not a copper. This is where we wash ourselves, Eliza.

ELIZA. You expect me to get into that and wet myself all over. Not me. I should catch my death. I knew a woman did it every Saturday night; and she died of it.

MRS PEARCE. Mr Higgins has the gentleman's bathroom downstairs; and he has a bath every morning, in cold water.

ELIZA. Ugh! He's made of iron, that man.

MRS PEARCE. If you are going to sit with him and with the Colonel, and be taught, you will have to do the same. They wont like the smell of you if you dont. But you can have the water as hot as you like. There are two taps, hot and cold.

ELIZA [weeping] I couldnt. I durstnt. Its not natural: it'ud kill me. Ive never had a bath in my life — not what youd call a proper one.

MRS PEARCE [kindly] Eliza: dont you want to be sweet and clean and decent, like a lady? You know

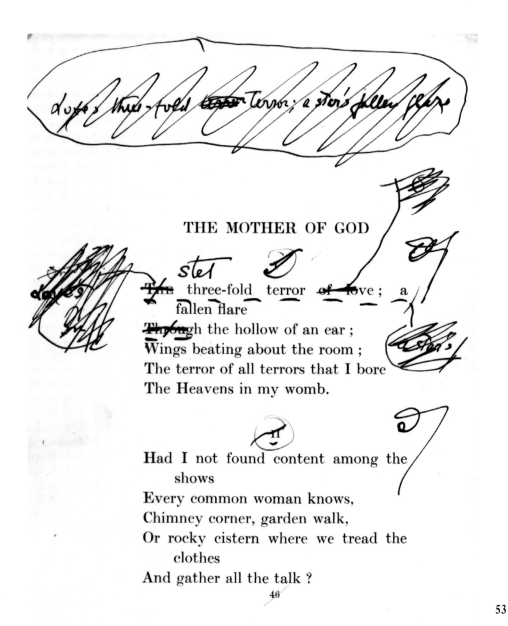

## THE MOTHER OF GOD

The three-fold terror of love; a
fallen flare
Through the hollow of an ear;
Wings beating about the room;
The terror of all terrors that I bore
The Heavens in my womb.

Had I not found content among the
shows
Every common woman knows,
Chimney corner, garden walk,
Or rocky cistern where we tread the
clothes
And gather all the talk?

40

53

**52** George Bernard Shaw (1856–1950): *Pygmalion.*
Shaw wrote over fifty plays, of which several were made into films; *Pygmalion*, first
performed in London in 1916, was among the most popular. This manuscript, in pencil and
red ink, is a film script written by Shaw in 1934.
[Add. MS 50628, f.20]

**53** William Butler Yeats (1865–1939): 'The Mother of God'.
Yeats's later poems achieve a spare, lilting lyricism far removed from the dense and elaborate
works of the 1890s. This is a proof, corrected and annotated by the author, of a poem from
*The Winding Stair and Other Poems*, published in 1933.
[Add. MS 55878, f.27v]

Eight said Big Ben, nine, ten eleven; & then with a roar
of finality, though presumably the strokes were accurately
spaced, all the last no more emphatic than the first
Twelve.

Always that — always that mystery, that fascination, that
glimpse withdrawn. But whose fault was it, she asked,
as Big Ben began striking One, Two, Three; &
she felt she was extraordinarily happy. She felt no
pity for the young man who had killed himself; none for her
self; none for herself; nothing but pride, nothing but
joy; for to hear Big Ben strike Three, Four,
Five, Six, Seven, was profound & tremendous, hearing
too that as she stood there, motor hoot & bus pass, or then
some sudden strange cry; while at her behind her in
the drawing room, people chattered, thanked, laughed;
she must go back; she must meant her enemy, she
must take her rose, Never would she submit —
never, never!

Eight, Big Ben struck, nine, ten, eleven; —

But Clarissa was gone.

54 Virginia Woolf (1882–1941): *Mrs Dalloway*.
The events of this novel, published in 1925, take place
within a single day, and are punctuated by Big Ben's
striking of the hours. It is an experiment in a new way
of writing which, through indirect narration and poetic
impressionism, illuminates the characters' inner lives.
This working draft dates from 1924.

[Add. MS 51046. f.99]

55 Virginia Woolf (1882–1941): *A Sketch of the Past*.
This typescript memoir, which includes an
unpublished study of Virginia Woolf's father Leslie
Stephen, was written between 19 June and 15
November 1940. The pencilled words in the left-hand
margin, clarifying the author's hasty scrawl, are in the
hand of her husband Leonard.

[Add. MS 61973, f.12]

an intellectual man, but still a man of that well to do sociable
late Victorian world. When he and my mother drive off in their
hansom which Amy has whistled off the rank, standing out in the
street in her cap and apron and giving two shrill blasts till the
hansom comes trotting--sometimes two handsoms raced each other
and disputed which had come first-- when they descend the many
steps anthahnxx from the front door to the street, he passes beyond
my horizon. I have never met anyone who knew my father in
evening dress; I have never met him in memoirs even. Yet he had great
charm for women, and was often attracted , as ⊥ could tell from
something gallant and tender in his manner, by the young and lovely.
The name of an American, Mrs Grey, comes back to me, and my mother
        somehow conveying to me that ⊥ might tease him , as ⊥ extricated
crumbs from his beard, about "flirting with pretty ladies."
Those were the words ⊥ used; and he looked at me not angry, for ⊥ was
only acting a parrot; still I remember the sudden shock, then he
 controlled what might have been a  snort; and said something
emphatic, as if to show me that he would stand no jokes about
that. There succeeds to that shock a memory of the immense
emphasis, with which once, when we were disputing were mothers eyes
large or small; "Your mothers eyes are the most beautiful in the
world." All the same ⊥ like to remember, for it gives humanity
to his austere figure that he was so struck, so normally and
masculinely affected by Mrs Langtrys beauty that he actually
went to the play to see her. Otherwise he never went to the play;
never went to picture galleries; had no ear whatsoever for music---
when Joachim played at Little Holland House he asked, when is it
going to begin'--the Beethoven or the Mozart being to his ears

55

56

**56** Siegfried Sassoon (1886–1967): *Memoirs of a Fox – Hunting Man*.
With the exception of the last two sections, which describe Sassoon's brutal
new life in the army during the First World War, his fictionalised
autobiography, published in 1928, recalls an idyllic childhood 'world of
simplicities'. This is the first of three notebooks containing the original draft:
the photograph on the left-hand page is of the author's mother.
[Add. MS 62547A, ff.8v–9]

**57** Wilfred Owen (1893–1918): 'Dulce et Decorum Est'.
Most of the poems for which Owen is remembered were written as a soldier in
the trenches, in an extraordinary burst of creativity between the summer of
1917 and his death in the autumn of the following year. The manuscripts were
edited by his friend and fellow poet Siegfried Sassoon, who published a
selection, including this famous poem, in 1920.
[Add. MS 43720, f.21]

# Dulce et Decorum est.

Bent double, like old beggars under sacks,

Knock-kneed, coughing like hags, we cursed through sludge,

Till on the haunting flares we turned our backs

And towards our distant rest began the trudge.

Some ~~New~~ marched asleep. ~~Many~~ had lost their boots

But limped on, blood-shod. All went lame; all blind;

~~Deaf even~~ Drunk with fatigue; deaf even to the hoots

Of ~~tired~~ ~~outstripped~~ ~~Five-Nines~~ ~~gas shells~~ that dropped behind.

gas shells dropping softly

Then somewhere near in front: Whew... fup, fop, fup,

Gas. shells? Or duds? We loosened masks in case, —

And listened. ~~Nothing~~. Far ~~no~~ rumouring of Krupp.

Then ~~sudden~~ poisons ~~but~~ us in the face.

Gas! GAS! Quick, boys! — An ecstasy of fumbling,

Fitting the clumsy helmets just in time;

But someone still was yelling out and stumbling,

And flound'ring like a man in fire or lime ...

Dim, through the misty panes and thick green light,

As under a green sea, I saw him drowning.

57

Dark branches of the pine encircle me
With sibilant insistence of the sea
While wrack & resin scent alternately
    The air I breathe
On slate compounded before man began
The racing ramparts of a spring tide ran
Below Bray Hill & yeasty in the sun
    They burst & seethe

A million years of unrelenting tide
~~Have smoothed the strata of the steep cliff side~~
Have smoothed & *clothed* the slate...
The purple slate with green & purple stretched...
A million million mar... sand rocks called,
    To shape these hills

Hot life pulsating, on the foreshore
One day the mayfly's life, three weeks the slugs
The woodworm's four year cycle burst its eggs
The flattened centipede ... its legs
    An & strive & kills

Hot life pulsating, on this foreshore dry
Damp life upshooting, from the marsh nearby
Onward on barrows dark against the sky
    The worn up dead?
... climb the steep ... height
Time's treasury ... in ... yet
... night behind me & before me night
    Where am I led?

( This is about the
    life & death of
    us )
    1966

**58** John Betjeman (1906–1984): 'By the Ninth Green, St Enodoc'. Betjeman was buried in the church of St Enodoc, in Cornwall, where he had worshipped throughout his life; the nearby golf-course was one of his favourite places. This is an untitled draft of a poem first published in 1966. The page is torn from a ruled foolscap ledger and crumpled as if rescued from the wastepaper-basket.

[Add. MS 54168 B, f.1]

**59** Wystan Hugh Auden (1907–1973): 'Down There'. This draft, from one of Auden's working notebooks, of a poem included in *About the House* (1966), dates from 1964. It is part of a poem cycle describing the farmhouse at Kirchstetten, near Vienna, which was his summer home from 1958 until his death. The stress marks indicate his intense concern with metre and rhythm.

[Add. MS 53772, f.63v]

58

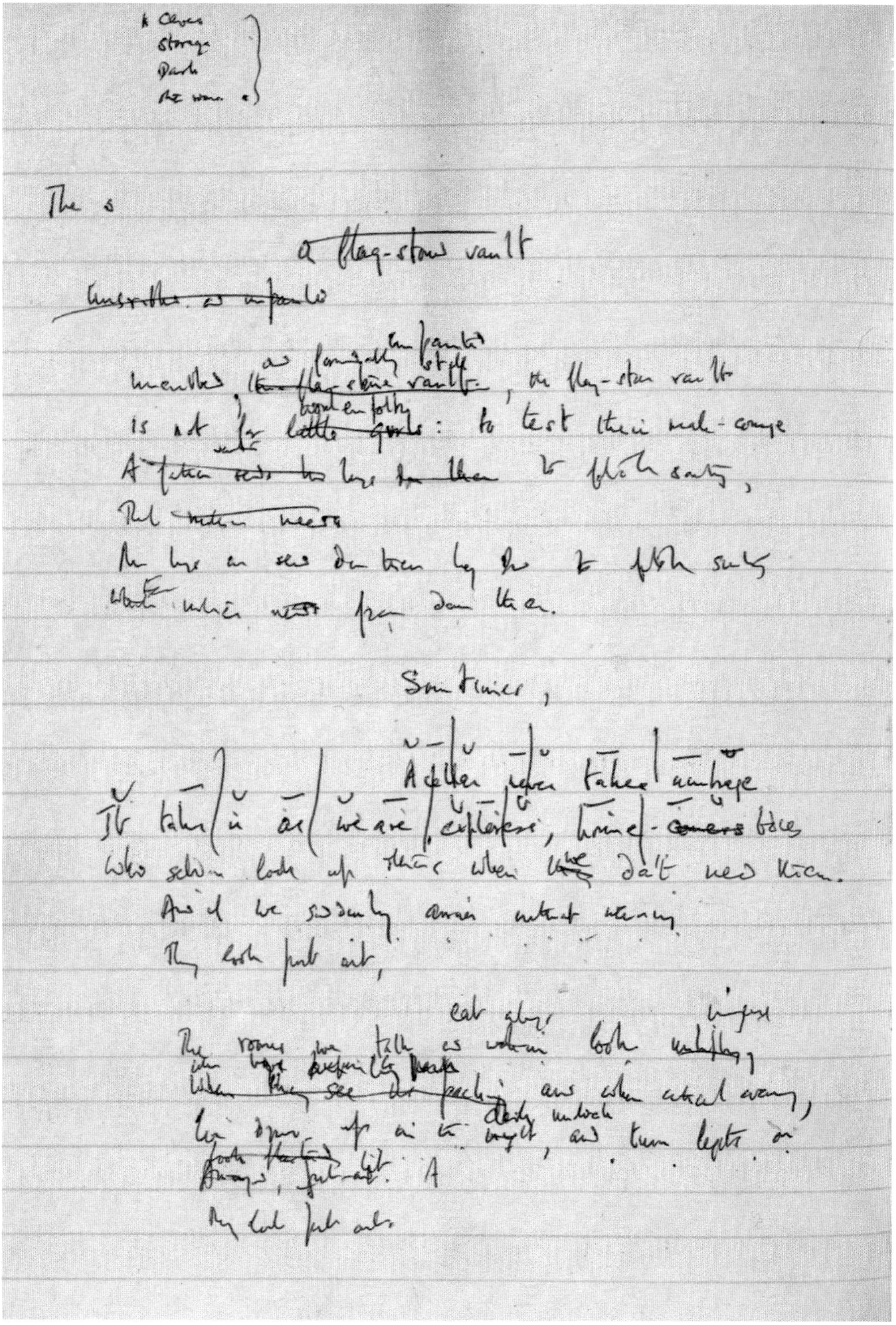

A Clever
storage
Dark
Re won

The s

a flag-stone vault

Inscribed as unfouled

Inscribed the flag-stone vault, the flag-stone vault
is not for little girls: to test their male-courage
A future seats too large than to flesh anting,
Phil matter meets
An log an see don tren by be to flesh surly
Most which west from dam the an.

Sometimes,

A clatter place takes umbrage
It takes in as we are, explorers, home-comers faces
who seldom look up their when they dai't med throw.
And if be suddenly amor without warning
They look push out,

eat glass           upset
The rooms me talk as whom look unstifling,
When they see don pecking aus when actual every
his dynamo up in it might, and turn lights or
looks thartend, bit. A
dashly unlock
by look just ants

59

My own news is very big and simple. I was married three days ago; to Caitlin Macnamara; in Penzance registry office; with no money, no prospect of money, no attendant friends or relatives, and in complete happiness. We've been meaning to from the first day we met, and now we are free and glad. We're moving next week — for how long depends on several things, but mostly on one — to a studio some miles away, in Newlyn, a studio above a fish-market & where gulls fly in to breakfast. But I shall be trying to come home soon for at least a few days, along with Caitlin; I think you'll like very much, she looks like the princess on the top of a Christmas tree, or like a stage Wendy; but, for God's sake, don't tell her that.
Write as soon as you can, and bless me.
Love to all the family.

Yours always,
Dylan

**60** Dylan Thomas
(1914–1953): Letter to
Vernon Watkins.
A collection of Dylan
Thomas's letters to Watkins,
a close friend, critic, admirer
and fellow poet, was
published after his death.
Watkins wrote that they
seemed to him 'the richest
letters of our time'. This one,
written from Mousehole,
Cornwall, on 15 July 1937,
quickly dispenses with the
usual intense poetic
discussion, having (in the
paragraph illustrated here)
greater news to impart.
[Add. MS 52612, f.5]

**62** Keith Douglas
(1920–1944): Pen and ink
sketch for *Alamein to Zem
Zem*.
When the Second World War
broke out, Douglas enlisted,
was eventually called up and
embarked for the Middle
East, where he gave up a staff
job in order to join his
regiment in the desert. He
described his experiences of
tank warfare in the
posthumously published
*Alamein to Zem Zem* (1946),
which was illustrated with his
own sketches.
[Add. MS 53775 A, f.63]

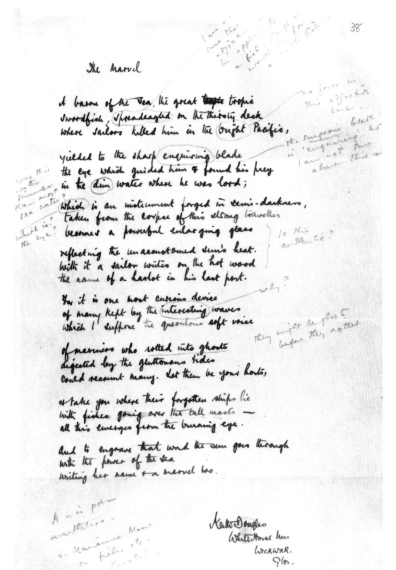

**61** Keith Douglas (1920–1944): 'The Marvel'.
The pencilled comments on this fair copy are by T. S. Eliot, who had been
introduced to Douglas's work by Edmund Blunden, his tutor at Oxford.
Douglas sent Eliot the poem in May 1941; it had been written earlier that
month while he was attending a gunnery course with his squadron at Linney
Head in Wales.
[Add. MS 53773, f.38]

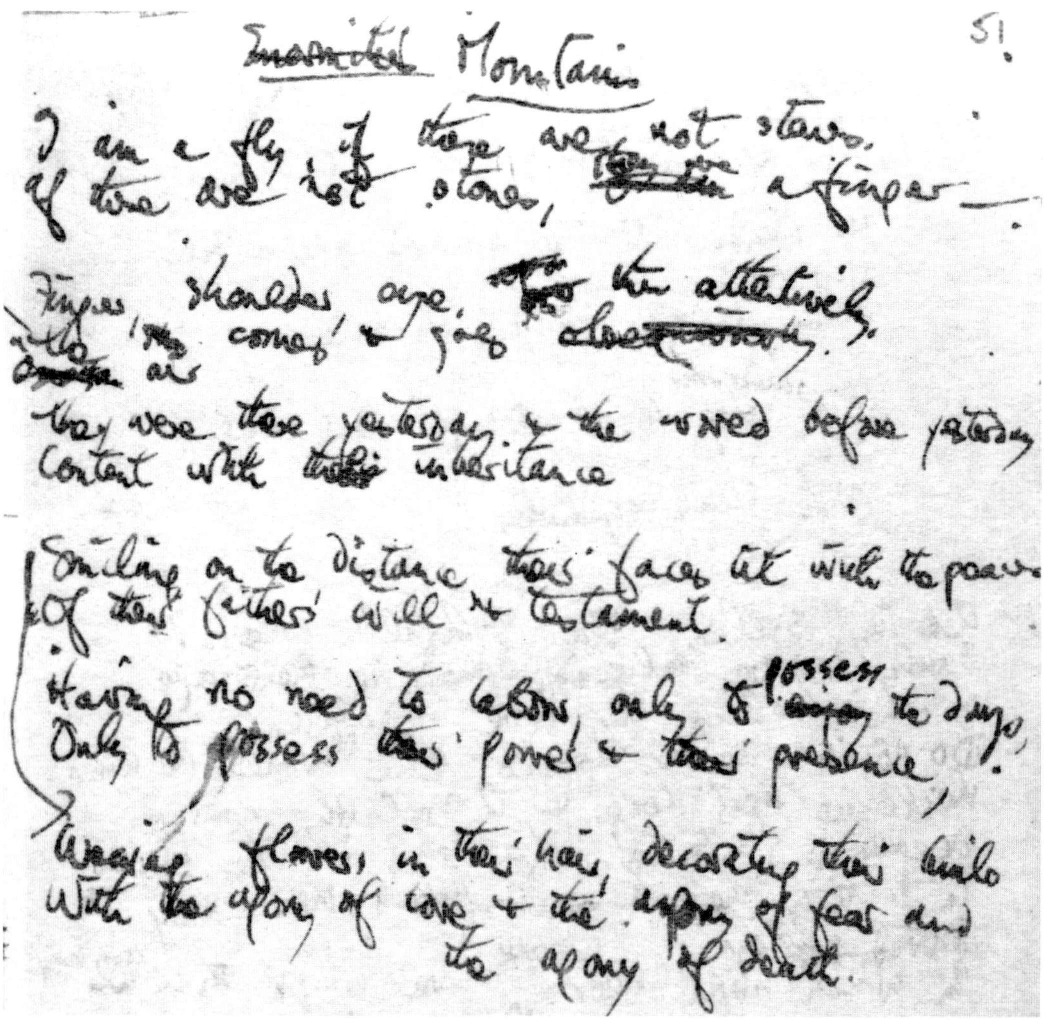

*[Handwritten poem draft, title: "Enamelled Mountains" (struck through to "Mountains")]*

*I am a fly if there are not stones,*
*If there are not stones, ... a finger —*

*Fingers, shoulders, eyes, ... the attentively*
*... comes ... going ...*

*they were there yesterday & the word before yesterday*
*Content with their inheritance*

*Smiling on to distance, their faces lit with the power*
*Of their fathers' will & testament.*

*Having no need to labour only to possess to days,*
*Only to possess their power & their presence,*

*Wearing flowers in their hair, decorating their hair*
*With the agony of love & the agony of fear and*
*the agony of death.*

**63** Ted Hughes (1930– ): 'Mountains'.
Hughes's acute sense of the beauty and the violence of the natural world
emerges in his earliest work. This corrected draft – an arrow indicates the final
order of the lines – is of a poem originally entitled 'Enormities', published in
*Wodwo*, 1967.
[Add. MS 53784, f.51]

Sylvia Plath

Three o'clock. The snorers & the deep, even breathers
Lie sunk in dreams or in oblivion,
lucky pebbles at the black bottom of a well.
So he imagines them - a city of pebbles.
~~The obdurate strip unwinds from spool to spool.~~
The incessant heat-lightning flicker of situations
Does not let up, or glow any more palatable
His mind hangs helpless as ~~a switch~~ the sky, or a sheet of laundry –
The cats have been howling like damaged instruments.
~~Among the aluminium ~~~~ of the tech cans.~~

Today & yesterday are two grey mirrors
He is intimate with fatigue, the shadowy lover
Who nightly, with great affection, peels back his skin.
She ~~sets~~ set his nerve-ends smoking like Vesuvius.
the mind hangs helpless as a ~~~~ sheet of paper,
Exhausted by the images that ~~swarm~~ on it.
~~she is indefensible ~~~~ fondues of the ~~~~
~~Whichever way he turns, he ~~~~ her arms,
~~As he sifts the life from him like ~~~~
But fatigue never she ~~keeps him awake by~~ her tireless whisperings
leaves the stumps in her arms like a ~~~~ of sand.

His ~~brain~~ head is like an interior of grey mirrors.
~~Each~~ gesture flees immediately down an alley
Of diminishing perspectives & its significance
Drains like water out the hole at the end.
He is plagued by the unlocatable desire, the repetition.
~~His eyes are lidless~~ Day & night ~~he must~~ bear witness
To the incessant, heat-lightning flicker of situations
The bald slots of his eyes ~~~~

**64** Sylvia Plath (1932–1963): 'Insomniac'.
Like many of Sylvia Plath's better known poems, 'Insomniac' evokes, in
extraordinarily vivid detail, a disturbed state of mind. It was completed in May
1961 and won a prize at the Cheltenham Festival that summer. These two
heavily-revised stanzas were discarded in the final version.
[Add. MS 52617, f.81]

# Song: The Three Ships

I saw three ships go sailing by
Over the sea, the lifting sea,
And the wind ~~blew~~ rose in the morning sky
And ~~they were~~ one was rigged for a long journey.

The first ship turned towards the west
Where the veins of gold lay
~~For there was gold to be where much gold~~ ~~possessed~~ ~~possessed~~ possessed.
~~....................~~ ~~....................~~

The second turned towards the east,
To countries where the mind grew clear
~~....................~~
And the greatest seemed the least;
~~It~~ And it was anchored in a year.
~~And it was rigged for a long journey.~~

The third ship drove towards the north
Over the sea, the darkening sea,
And ~~....................~~ the snow and ice came forth,
And the ropes shone frostily.

lay harsh and
The northern sky ~~grey~~ ~~stormily~~ black
Over the sad unfruitful sea,
East and west the ships came back
~~....................~~ Happily or unhappily.

~~But~~ The third drove farther on
Into an ~~unforgiving sea~~
~~....................~~ where a strange ~~....................~~ light shone
And it was rigged for a long journey.

8. x. 44.

# Suggestions for further reading

**65** Philip Larkin (1922–1985): 'Song: The Three Ships'. Larkin's early poems were, by his own account, greatly influenced by Yeats. This is a notebook draft, dated 8 October 1944, of 'Legend', the opening section of the title poem of his first collection, *The North Ship*, published in 1945.
[Add. MS 52619, f.3]

Lewis Carroll (Charles Lutwidge Dodgson) (1832–1898): the 'mouse's tail' poem from *Alice's Adventures under Ground*.
[Add. MS 46700, f.15v]

## English Literature

*The Oxford Companion to English Literature* ed. Margaret Drabble, Oxford University Press, 1985.

George Sampson *The Concise Cambridge History of English Literature* 3rd edn., Cambridge, 1970.

## Handwriting of English Literary Manuscripts

Giles Dawson and Laetitia Kennedy-Skipton *Elizabethan Handwriting* London: Faber, 1968.

P. J. Croft *Autograph Poetry in the English Language* 2 vols., London: Cassell, 1973.

L. C. Hector *The Handwriting of English Documents* London: Arnold, 1958.

A. G. Petti *English Literary Hands from Chaucer to Dryden* London: Arnold, 1977.

Verlyn Klinkenborg, Herbert Cahoon and Charles Ryskamp *British Literary Manuscripts* Series I (800–1800) and II (1800–1914), New York: Pierpont Morgan Library and Dover Publications Inc., 1981.

## English Literary Manuscripts

*Index of English Literary Manuscripts* London: Mansell, 1980–. Volumes so far published are Vol.I, 1450–1625, ed. Peter Beal, 2 parts, 1980; Vol.III, 1700–1800, Part I, Addison-Fielding, ed. Margaret M. Smith, 1986; and Vol.IV, 1800–1900, Part I, Arnold-Gissing, ed. Barbara Rosenbaum and Pamela White, 1982.

## Facsimiles

Early English Text Society: *Beowulf* (no.245, 2nd edn., 1959); *Sir Gawain* (no.162, 1923); and *The Winchester Malory* (Suppl. Series no.4, 1976).

University of Leeds Studies in English, Mediaeval Drama Facsimiles, no.IV: *N-Town Plays* (1977).

D. Thomas and Jane Cox *Shakespeare in the Public Records* London: H.M.S.O., 1985.

*The Notebook of William Blake* ed. D. V. Erdman, Oxford, 1973 (rev. edn., New York, 1977).

*The Manuscript of Wordworth's 'Poems, in Two Volumes' (1807)* ed. W. H. Kelliher, London: British Library Publications, 1984.

Jane Austen *The Manuscript Chapters of 'Persuasion'* ed. R. W. Chapman, 1926, repr. London: Athlone Press, 1985.

Lewis Carroll *Alice's Adventures Under Ground* London: Pavilion Books, 1985.

T. S. Eliot *The Waste Land* ed. Valerie Eliot, London: Faber, 1971.

*The James Joyce Archive* [including facsimiles of *Finnegan's Wake* and the *Ulysses* note-sheets in the British Library], New York: Garland Press, 1977–1979.

disgrace to humanity, that pest of society, Elizabeth. Many were the people who fell Martyrs
to the protestant Religion during her reign;
I suppose not fewer than a dozen. She mar-
-ried Philip King of Spain who in her Sister's
reign for famous for building Armadas. She died
without issue, & then the dreadful moment came
in which the destroyer of all comfort, the deceitful
Betrayer of trust reposed in her, & the Murderess of
her Cousin succeeded to the Throne. ——

Elizabeth ——

Elizabeth.

Mrs. D. I. Lotts.